CW00499272

# ALL THE WAY TO MEMPHIS
## THE STORY OF
# MOTT THE HOOPLE

### BY PHILIP CATO

S.T. PUBLISHING

*For Sea Divers Everywhere . . .*

All The Way To Memphis - The Story Of Mott The Hoople (pbk)

© Philip Cato, 1997

ISBN  1 898927 60 X

Published by S.T. Publishing, Scotland.
Printed by Victoria Press, England.

All rights reserved.  No part of  this publication may be reproduced, stored in a retrieval system, or transmitted, in any form or by any means, without the prior permission in writing from the publisher, nor be otherwise circulated in any form of binding or cover other than that in which it is  published and without a similar condition including this condition being imposed on the subsequent purchaser.  In short, take the piss and we send the boys round.

A CIP catalogue record for this book is available from the British Library.

Extra special mentions and thanks have to be given to the following: Terry Greenhalf and his 'Once Bitten' club and Sven Gusevik and his *Outsider* fanzine, the source of the tour dates plus the Dale Griffin anecdotes.  Both operations have now sadly ceased to exist, but their tireless work and devotion in the past to keeping the name of this great band alive deserves drinks all round!  Last but not least my heartfelt appreciation to Ray Waters, Mandy Jeffcock, Andy Smith and Malcolm Walsh in England and Justin Purington in America for the countless hours of live recordings they have supplied me with.  Their faith in the band and trust in me is sincerely appreciated.  Here's to many more hours happy listening.  Thanks also to my old mate and fellow Mott fan, Ted Carroll.  Oh, and lest we forget.  Hats off to Morgan, Mick, Pete, Verden, Dale, Ian, Guy, Luther, Bowie and Ronno for making it all happen (not forgetting Stan and the roadies!).  Without you, the Seventies just wouldn't have been the same.  Cheers lads, all the best!

Front cover photo by Barry Plummer

The following books proved invaluable:
BOWIE: Jerry Hopkins (Corgi)
MAKING TRACKS: Charlie Gillett (Panther)
THE DAVID BOWIE STORY: George Tremlett (Futura)
SHOTS FROM THE HIP: Charles Shaar Murray (Penguin)
RARE RECORD GUIDE 1995: Record Collector (Diamond)
ALIAS DAVID BOWIE: Peter & Leni Gillman (Hodder & Stoughton)
DIARY OF A ROCK'N'ROLL STAR: Ian Hunter (Panther)
BEFORE I GET OLD: Dave Marsh (Plexus)
HAMMER OF THE GODS: Stephen Davies (Ballentine)
BOOK OF ROCK STARS (Guinness)
PSYCHOTIC REACTIONS & CARBURETTOR DUNG: Lester Bangs (Minerva)
I have also plundered the archives of the following publications:
*Circus, Creem, Disc, NME, Fusion, International Times, Sounds, Mojo, Q Magazine, Melody Maker, Zoo World, Crawdaddy, Diana, Let It Rock, Record Mirror, Record Collector* and *Beat Instrumental*.

## S.T. Publishing

P.O. Box 12, Lockerbie, Dumfriesshire. DG11 3BW. Bonnie Scotland.

INTEGRITY. That's the word. In his classic book on the band, *Diary Of A Rock'N'Roll Star*, Ian Hunter promises the reader that "I'll begin at the beginning andI will write as simply as I can because I want people to read it as it happens". Over 20 years later, as I embarked on a journey that would take me through dozens of books, piles of magazines, folders full of clippings, and hours upon hours of recordings (both bootleg and legit), I found those few words echoing around my head. I recalled those heady days in the early Seventies - days full of cars, clothes, girls and teenage optimism. But most of all I remember the music, blasting from the battered old Dansette my mother kept tucked away in the front room. Originally purchased second hand to play the platters of Jim Reeves and Perry Como, it now vibrated to the tunes of a whole new bunch of bad boys. Bowie, Rod & The Faces, The New York Dolls, plus a host of classic Northern Soul platters all battling for needle time on the dusty old turntable.

My Mum even went as far as letting me play the odd track from *Raw Power*, as long as the next door neighbours were out at the time. But there was one band she couldn't stand. Not because they looked odd (well, not compared to Bowie, Iggy and Johnny Thunders anyway), and not because they couldn't play in tune (that was Ronnie Woods' job). No, it was simply down to the fact that they, more than any of the others, sang songs about violence, disruption, boredom, and about just not taking it anymore. To a middle-aged housewife raised in the quiet confines of the rural Midlands, listening to Mott The Hoople was tantamount to torching the Union Jack in the middle of the front lawn. She never missed a chance to tell me that "they're nothing but a load of old rubbish", genuinely believing in her heart of hearts that her spotty faced 13 year old would eventually see the light and come 'round to her way of thinking.

Oh, how little she knew of the inner workings of the teenage mind. Like countless other rebels without a cause, kicking their heels in anticipation of a revolution that would never come, this was just what I wanted to hear. Talk about tossing a Molotov onto the fire! If my mother hates them, my teenage space cadet logic told me, they must be cool.

And so it was that I embarked on a journey, scoffing at the teenyboppers with their Rollers and Partridge Family, while brushing off the taunts of sixth-formers who thought that if an album didn't have four sides, at least a dozen 15 minute organ solos and a front cover by Roger Dean, then it wasn't worth owning, let alone spending countless hours in your tiny bedroom pouring over Ian Hunter's lyrics about urban decay and Times Square hustlers.

A couple of years later, having left school behind, I scraped enough money together to Skytrain it over to New York, only to find it was exactly as Ian had described it. The seedy and the snazz, the shoeboys and the satins.

So, like Ian, I don't intend this book "to have literary merit, nor to be a journalist's delight". It's simply a story by a fan for a fan. I've tried to keep it simple and I've tried to keep it straight. All I hope is that it jogs a few memories and gets you out there again amongst the record racks. After all, it's a mighty long way down rock'n'roll, and the way I see it, we ain't even half way there yet. Oh, and one more thing . . . THANKS MUM.

Philip Cato.

*"I knew Guy had a large record collection, so when I opened The Scene I offered him Monday nights. And it was absolutely immaculate. He would announce every record, tell you who it was and where it was from. He used to carry the records around in a huge trunk, and he was so protective of them that he used to sit on top of it while he dj'd. I've even seen him sleep on it. It was like a religion to him, it really was."*
*RONAN O'RAHILLY.*

*"There are only two Phil Spectors in this world, and I am one of them."*
*GUY STEVENS.*

## CHAPTER

# 1

Guy Stevens was an accident waiting to happen. A walking talking chemistry class, orange haired and stick-insect thin, the archetypal punk kid on the make who kissed goodbye to a life of quiet desperation in the suburbs and headed on down the highway that led to the bright lights of the big city in search of some real action. Looking like an extra from a Colin McInnes novel, he took his lead from Kerouac's *On The Road*, playing the part of the book's main motorhead, Neal Cassady, with the steely determination and wanton abandonment found only in the most truly possessed.

In the spring of '59, just turned seventeen, he had come to London, scored some lowly paid job with an anonymous City institution, and dived headfirst into the rock'n'roll pool that had sprung up since Cliff's *Move It* first charted the previous November. He wasted no time in finding a girlfriend (soon to be Mrs Diane Stevens) who, in a classic case of understatement, remembered that "he had an interest in rock'n'roll. We went to every Jerry Lee Lewis concert ever. Then he became quite obsessional and started chasing things like *Money* by Barrett Strong, going all over London to shops he thought might have it. I don't know how he knew where the shops were, but he did . . . if you really want something you do, don't you? It became his life." It was this almost paranoid fixation with hard to find vinyl that led him to Ronan O'Rahilly, founding father of Radio Caroline and, at the time, owner of a little club located at 41 Great Windmill Street, which he had christened The Scene. O'Rahilly, already something of a thorn in the side of the Establishment due to his antics on the high seas, had picked up the lease on the cheap in December, 1962, from Giorgio Gomelsky, who had struggled for some time to make ends meet running it as The Piccadilly. At that time Gomelsky was a 29 year old Russian whose family had fled to Switzerland to escape the Nazis during the war. In the mid Fifties, Gomelsky had moved to London where an interest in jazz had led him to Chris Barber and The National Jazz League. The two quickly became friends, and Barber, who had a sideline interest booking American Blues singers, got Gomelsky a job acting as road manager to the visiting artists. In the early Sixties, Gomelsky branched out into film making, but his interest in music led him to open The Piccadilly which had formerly operated as the Cy Laurie Folk Cellar.

After The Piccadilly closed its doors for the last time, Gomelsky pitched camp in Richmond, an area he knew well from his days with Barber (the National Jazz League's first festival was held at the Richmond Athletic sports ground), and took up an offer from the landlord of the Station Hotel in Kew Road to try his hand at livening up what was traditionally a slow Sunday night. Taking over the hotel's large backroom, Gomelsky opened The Crawdaddy Club (named after the Bo Diddley song, *Do The Crawdaddy*) and began trawling for talent. The first act to tread the boards was The Dave Hunt Band, a rockin' little combo heavily influenced by Louis Jordan, who had amongst their ranks a skinny, spotty faced guitarist called Ray Davies. Mr. Hunt and his boys went down a storm with the locals and soon secured a regular gig at the club. However, it was during a particularly harsh winter evening in December, '62, that Gomelsky received a call informing him that the band's van was snowbound somewhere on the A1 and they wouldn't be able to make the show. Needing a replacement act in a hurry, Gomelsky remembered a ramshackle R&B covers band who had once gigged at The Piccadilly after being thrown out of The Marquee. Gomelsky knew they lived locally and a couple of phonecalls later he located their pianist Ian Stewart at his desk job at nearby I.C.I. By 7.30 that evening, The Rollin' Stones (as they were then calling themselves) hit the stage to a somewhat shell-shocked audience. Gomelsky loved them, offered to be their manager, and the rest, as they say, is history.

Meanwhile, back at The Scene, O'Rahilly was so knocked out by Stevens' knowledge of music and his massive collection of obscure American 45s, that he offered him a job as d.j. on Monday evenings. It wasn't long before the venue had become a major stopping-off point for members of the rapidly burgeoning mod movement. Former first-class ticket, Pete Shuster, a regular at the Stevens' sessions, remembered the club as "one squarish room, with the d.j. in the corner, and a bar where you could get an expresso or a soft drink in the other. All you could do was dance; there wasn't room for anything else. But the music was the main thing we went for, the fact that Guy Stevens was the d.j. He played the kind of things people wanted to hear, and couldn't hear anywhere else."

Stevens' growing reputation as a turntable wizard finally curtailed any thoughts of conventional employment and, coupled with The Scene's virtual overnight rise to fame as ground control for Mod Central, elevated him to the status of cult hero. Years later he would recall that "by '63 I had all these records that I'd imported from Sam's Record Store in Shreveport, Louisiana . . . and Peter Meaden came 'round one night." Meaden, something of an ace face on the mod scene, had, through his struggling PR business, come into contact with a bunch of teenagers from Acton who called themselves The Detours. Deciding that it would be a smart move to hitch a ride on the mod bandwagon, Meaden talked the band into changing their name to The High Numbers, in those days a slang term for stylish dressers. Meaden explained to Stevens that the band, while having all the attributes of first class musicians, were woefully short of suitable material.

Stevens invited the boys around to his flat, sat them down in the tiny living room, made them a cup of tea, and then "played 'em *Rumble* by Link Wray, and put it on tape for them, because by then I'd built up this enormous collection, and Steve Marriot (of the soon to be mod sensations, The Small Faces) and everybody used to come round to get material."

Indeed, Marriot had been an early disciple of Stevens. A former child actor (he had appeared in *Dixon Of Dock Green* and *Mr. Pastry,* and starred in the Peter Sellers' film, *Heavens Above*), Marriot had turned his attentions to music, using the Stevens' connection as a springboard to stardom. At the time of Meadon's visit, he was working as a shop assistant at the J60 Music Bar in Manor Park High Street, and had cut one unsuccessful single *Give Her My Regards* b/w *Imaginary Love* for Decca, although a chance meeting with a band called The Outcasts, featuring Kenney Jones and Ronnie Lane, would soon change his life dramatically. Spotted by pop svengali, Don Arden, they were signed to Decca and, as The Small Faces, became the most important band in the history of mod.

Pete Meaden had heard that Guy Stevens would, for a sum of £5, make up tapes from his extensive (as well as expensive) record collection. Handing over the necessary readies, he took the two and a half hour tape back home. Included in the selection were Slim Harpo's *Got Love If You Want It* and The Showmen's *Country Fool* (the flip side of their 1962 single, *It Will Stand,* on London Records) which, after a little creative juggling, re-emerged as *I'm The Face* and *Zoot Suit,* The High Numbers' debut 45.

Before long the word was out on the little guy with the encyclopaedic knowledge of obscure R&B and, as Ronan O'Rahilly remembers, before long "everybody would come to hear Guy. The Stones, The Beatles, Eric Clapton, all the major stars. People would come from all over the country on Monday nights, and from France and Holland too. It was that good."

In January, 1964, Guy founded The Chuck Berry Fan Club, and later that month took it upon himself to fly to the States to meet Berry upon his release from jail, where he had been resident as a guest of the Indiana Federal Prison since February, 1962, the rap being a violation of the Mann Act, which prohibits transportation of minors across State lines for immoral purposes. Berry violated the law when he recruited Janice Escalante, a 14 year old Apache Indian, bringing her from El Paso to work as a hat-check girl at The Bandstand, a club he owned in downtown St. Louis. It later emerged that Miss Escalante was a hooker and, although he eventually fired her, Chuck was forced to take a fall. Stevens told Ian Hunter some years later that both he and Don Arden were waiting at the prison gates for Berry. Arden supposedly offered Chuck $10,000 to tour England, but Berry, notoriously sharp in all matters of a fiscal nature, turned him down and went with Stevens, who reckoned he had secured the rock'n'roll poet's services by doubling his rival's offer.

Like Hunter, Diane Stevens found this tale rather dubious, believing that it sounded "like a bit of self-mythology to me", although Dave Betteridge, later a colleague at Island Records, was amazed by Stevens' sheer nerve. "He went and met Chuck Berry and STAYED with Chuck Berry, one of the five most difficult people in the world to deal with. But he could see that Guy was a real fan and had a friendly relationship with him."

The tour, regardless of Stevens' offer, never took place (Chuck did visit Britain in May, '64, as part of a package show featuring Carl Perkins, The Animals, and The Nashville Teens) although his friendship with Berry afforded him a unique opportunity to hang out with the great man. In an *NME* interview 15 years later, Stevens told rock scribe Charles Shaar Murray that "I was at a session with Phil Chess in 1964 with Chuck Berry when he was doing *Nadine* and *Promised Land*. I was at the session. I was taking photographs . . . I put tremendous pressure on Pye Records, who had Chess and Checker over here, and the head of the company at the time was Ian Ralfini . . . I put pressure on him to get *Memphis Tennessee* released as a single. It was out as a b-side with *Let It Rock*. They taped all the Chuck Berry tracks off my records. Not from master tapes, but from my records. I mean, I may have spat on them or something. You never know what happens, do you? Now you'll know that if your old Chuck Berry records jump or something, it's probably me spitting on them."

Broke and back in Britain, Stevens was reduced to hustling Scene Club tickets to tourists outside Piccadilly Circus underground in order to make ends meet. It was here that he bumped into Chris Blackwell, the man who would change his life. Born in 1937 into the Crosse & Blackwell soup dynasty, young Christopher had been brought up in Jamaica, mostly at his father's mansion in Waterloo Road, in those days Kingston's smartest suburb. In 1947, he was sent to England for a Harrow education, and after graduating, he drifted into a job with accountant's Price Waterhouse, although legend has it he spent more time at the dog track than at his desk. Returning to the Caribbean in the late Fifties, he found employment firstly as an estate agent, then an aide-de-camp to the Governor General, followed by a spell as a water sports instructor at the Half Moon Bay Hotel in Montego Bay. It was during this period that Blackwell first came into contact with Rastafarians, a local religious sect he initially believed to be white hating killers, but later found to be laid back and friendly. Turned on by their music, he began hanging around the many sound systems then operating in downtown Kingston, which is where he first came into contact with the now legendary Clement 'Sir Coxsone' Dodd.

By 1959, the smooth talking Blackwell had charmed himself into a job as production assistant to film producer Harry Saltzman, who was on the island shooting the James Bond classic, *Doctor No*. Managing to get enough money together to enable him to quit his job (allegedly on the advice of a fortune teller), he founded Island Records, christening his label after the Alec Waugh novel, *Island In The Sun*. The label's first pressing was from a tape of the Half Moon Bay's house band backing Bermudan pianist Lance Haywood, although it would be 1961 before Laurel Aitken's *Little Sheila* gave Blackwell his first local hit.

Using the money from this record, he secured the distribution rights to Coxsone Dodd's productions, and by 1962 he could be found trawling the back streets of Brixton and Birmingham peddling bluebeat (as Jamaican ska was then known) 45s from the back of a beat up Mini Cooper. That same year he opened an office in London (located at 108 Cambridge Road, Kilburn Park) and scored the label's first U.K. hit with Owen Gray's dance cash-in, *Twist Baby*. It would be another two years before the big time hit however, when Millie Small's *My Boy Lollipop* sold a million copies thanks to a licensing deal with Fontana which got the records out of the boot of Blackwell's car and into the chart.

Twelve months earlier the young would-be tycoon had visited New York to strike up a distribution deal with Sue Records, which gave him first option on U.K. releases from their extensive R&B catalogue. Wishing to devote his own energies to developing Island, Blackwell had been on the lookout for a suitable manager for the British end of the Sue operation and, having heard on the grapevine about Stevens' formidable reputation as a trendsetter, he offered him the job at £15 a week. Naturally, given his rather reduced circumstances, Stevens was in like a shot, later telling the *NME* that "Sue was formed by a guy called Juggy Murray in New York, and he started the label with Charlie & Inez Foxx's *Mockingbird*. That was Sue 301. I went over and got a record called *The Love Of Man* by Viola Kilgare. Unbelievable. Blitzkrieg, out of the window, number one easy. He owned the copyright. Chris went over and offered him $500, but Juggy wanted half a million. It got to three in the American charts, if you check back you'll find it (for the record, the lady in question was Theola Kilgore, and the record reached 21 on the Billboard chart of November, 1963). One of the greatest records I've ever heard in my life. I wanted it to be on Sue. I wanted Bob Dylan to be on Sue. That was why I started importing records for Island with Dave and Chris. And it nearly bankrupted Island."

Dave Betteridge recalled that "the criterion for being on Sue was, did Guy like it? Did Guy think it had some musical relevance? From the American label we put out a few dozen singles like Jimmy McGriff (*All About My Girl*, *Last Minute Parts 1&2*, *I've Got A Woman Parts 1&2*, and *Round Midnight*), and then we developed into a fully fledged label which eventually had all sorts of things on it; Ike & Tina Turner, Betty Everett, Rufus Thomas, a huge spread of things. Guy never operated as an office guy; he was a burning flame. He had Chris on one side and me on the other and between us we managed to get him focused on the business. We made money on maybe one in five singles, like James Brown's *Night Train*. The pay off was the four volumes of *The Sue Story*; those sold over a long period of time."

While Sue ran from '63 to '67 as a totally off the wall operation, Chris Blackwell was concentrating his efforts into moving Island away from ska and bluebeat imports via a deal with Lee Gopthal which would see Jamaican sides issued on the Trojan label. Terminating his hit and miss deal with Fontana, he moved into the calmer waters of a distribution deal with the giant Philips organisation.

With Sue now effectively a lost cause, Stevens moved over to Island's A&R department. Former house producer and Spencer Davis Group bassist, Muff Winwood, recalled that "one day Chris came in and said, 'Great news, Guy is joining us tomorrow'. And we're all going 'Fucking hell' and holding our heads. So the next day we're sitting there and you can hear this kerfuffle getting nearer and nearer, and the door bursts open and Guy leaps up onto the table, hair everywhere, dressed in these amazingly tight skinny trousers and suede creepers, and shouts; 'We're gonna make this the best fucking record company in the world!' And he just jumped around from then on."

Manic behaviour notwithstanding, Dave Betteridge willingly conceded that "he was the guardian of Island's taste. He set the style and indicated the way Island, and companies like them, have continued to be."

Stevens had first tried his hand at record production during his time at Sue when he had recorded a live album featuring rocker Larry Williams (*Larry Williams On Stage*, released in 1965), but it was to be with Cumbrian band The VIPs that he first began to develop his soon to be legendary production techniques. Chris Blackwell had signed the band after seeing them support Island's number one act at the time, The Spencer Davis Group, at Hamburg's (in)famous Star Club, although they were put on hold for a while as Blackwell considered the teenage Stevie Winwood far more worthy of his attention. Eventually the job of recording the band was given to Stevens. He taped four songs which were issued as singles (*I Wanna Be Free* b/w *Don't Let Go* and *Straight Down To The Bottom* b/w *In A Dream*) and also used them to back artists Michael English and Nigel Weymouth (aka Hapdash & The Coloured Coat) on their now semi-legendary *Featuring The Human Host & The Heavy Metal Kids* album, although it would take a couple of personnel switches and a name change to Spooky Tooth before they would see any commercial success.

Stevens ranted on to the *NME* about "these blokes (who) came down from Carlisle in a van, and they were INCREDIBLY HEAVY, both physically and because they were all taking about 500 blues a week. I loved them. I thought they were incredible and I took Blackwell along to see them . . . the first thing I actually produced was with Spooky Tooth. It was called *In A Dream* and it BUILT UP. All my records build up. Have you noticed that? *Spooky Two* was THE ALBUM."

Stevens' next signing was a young blues combo from London who had began life as Black Cat Bones, an outfit based around drummer Simon Kirke and maverick guitarist Paul Kossoff. After numerous auditions they teamed up with former Brown Sugar vocalist Paul Rodgers and ex-John Mayall's Bluesbreakers bassist, fifteen year old Andy Fraser. At the suggestion of blues guru Alexis Korner, they began gigging as Free. Stevens was instantly taken in by their raw earthy sound, but thought their name was a little too similar to a band featuring drummer Ginger Baker and organist Graham Bond called Free At Last. In soon to be characteristic fashion, the producer suggested a name change to The Heavy Metal Kids, but the band stuck to their guns. Island's Tim Clark recalled that "he used to keep a little black book with names that he'd thought of. If he stumbled across a band and thought they were great but didn't like their name, he'd consult his little list to come up with something better."

Drummer Kirke remembered that "he wanted Free to be called The Heavy Metal Kids, which was actually way before its time. And also *Tons Of Sobs* (the band's debut album) - that was his. He was pretty knocked out with us, that we could turn on such a wailing, bluesy wall of sound, and it just triggered this phrase in him." Kirke was also suitably impressed with his producer's knowledge of music, remembering that "he turned us on to *The Basement Tapes*. He got hold of them years before anybody else and wanted Free to cover a couple of songs."

Another outfit to receive the Steven's treatment in 1968 were King Crimson, a band he talked Blackwell into signing even though their debut album for Deram had shifted less than 600 copies, and he also worked on the production for the sessions that would become the first album by Traffic, although the band turned down his suggestion of *Mad Shadows* as a title. But Stevens' main claim to fame at that time was the hand he had in the formation of Procol Harum, a band formed from the ashes of The Paramounts, a second division R&B combo who were all but ready to throw in the towel prior to meeting the producer. The band's lead singer Gary Brooker acknowledged that Stevens was "important in our development. We used to go 'round to Guy's house and he became a mate. He'd say 'Listen to this . . . yeah, very rare imports'. We always used to pinch a few songs and put them in our repertoire."

Indeed it was Stevens who initially put Brooker in touch with lyricist Keith Reid, who at the time was an occasional lodger at chez Stevens, upon which The Paramounts became The Pinewoods, a name Stevens hated. He suggested instead that they call themselves after a cat owned by a friend of his. The feline in question was called Procul Harum, Latin for "beyond these things". A minor spelling alteration and the band were up and running, although try as he might Stevens could not catch the attention of Chris Blackwell, who had the demo for what would eventually become *A Whiter Shade Of Pale* on his desk for a week. "What happened was this boy I knew called Keith Reid came into the office with these words he'd written. He worked in a solicitor's office for £4.50 a week, and he brought these words which were vaguely Dylanish, and I told him the words were great and suggested he got himself a good songwriter." Stevens then contacted Brooker and *A Whiter Shade Of Pale* became an instant classic, eventually selling over six million copies in Britain alone and knocking The Beatles' *All You Need Is Love* off the top spot in June, 1967 in the process. It also made a small fortune for Deram, the company that eventually released it.

By now Stevens had established himself as a proven spotter of talent, although it was obvious to those close to him that his once naturally manic behaviour was now being kick-started by massive doses of speed which, coupled with his unquenchable thirst for alcohol, began to make him increasingly accident prone. Dave Betteridge remembered that "we kept losing him. He'd go off on binges. He actually fell asleep in a hotel once and burned it down with an electric fire. It did become difficult. He wouldn't have lasted 20 minutes in any other company."

Further misfortune conspired to hit him hard when his prized collection of records was stolen from his mother's house. To add insult to injury the thief flogged the platters for nine pennies each. A shell-shocked Stevens believed that "the guy didn't know what he was selling. I had every Miracles record. Every Muddy Waters record. I had every Chess record from 001."

At this point Stevens could be forgiven for thinking that things couldn't get any worse, and that his share of bum breaks was well and truly over. But a minor bust in the summer of '68 for possession of cannabis resulted in a particularly harsh J.P. handing down a one year stretch in Wormwood Scrubs, home to some of Britain's most hardened criminals. Although he was eventually given time off for good behaviour, Dave Betteridge believed that "it didn't do him any good". In the long run this was probably true, but the immediate result was the opening of a whole new chapter of productivity, a phase in his life he acknowledged as being vitally important when he told *NME* that "I was doing eight months for possession of drugs and I read this book called *Mott The Hoople* by Willard Manus. I wrote to my wife and said 'Keep this title a secret' . . . she wrote back and said; 'Are you joking? Mott The Hoople? THAT'S RIDICULOUS!.'"

*"These young English boys in The Doc Thomas group, hailing from the county of Herefordshire, used little time in reaching a very high level of vocal / instrumental quality musicianship. They discovered the rhythm and blues style at a time other British groups were still playing the Liverpool sound. Their high quality vanguard beat music distinguishes them from the others. Their inspiration comes from soul music; that typical negro traditional rhythm and blues - thus gaining a personal style that stirs up great feelings and emotions in the audience. Doc Thomas Group translates their thoughts and feelings, bringing their image of love to the audience. It is no coincidence that their 'plantation song style' you hear in some of their songs recalls the golden age of the fabulous jazz years."*

ITALIAN SLEEVE NOTES.

**CHAPTER**

**2**

**In October, 1962, Parlophone released the debut British 45 by Merseyside beat combo The Beatles. The group had been kicking its heels in one form or another since the late Fifties, and although they had been regularly packing in the punters at Hamburg's Star Club and Liverpool's Cavern, they had been shown the door by almost every record company in the land. Finally they had scored a deal with EMI who, believing they were just a passing fad, tucked them away on their obscure Parlophone label, and delegated all production chores to label boss George Martin. The single, a catchy mid-tempo toetapper with an instantly infectious harmonica break called** *Love Me Do,* **received minimal promotion and almost zero airplay from the mighty BBC and, as a result, by Christmas it had stiffed at 17 on the chart.**

In January, '63, Parlophone followed it up with *Please Please Me*, although again expectations were not exactly running at fever pitch. But this time the disc, a far punchier and polished performance than its predecessor, caught the public's ears, and by February it was number one on the chart. By the summer of '63, the group had released an EP, *Twist And Shout*, which went to number two, the *Please Please Me* album which went to number one, and a third single, *She Loves You*, which hit the top spot on its second week of release.

This phenomenal success opened the floodgates for aspiring pop groups, and all over the country young men began picking up guitars and forming bands. From Newcastle emerged The Animals, Manchester had The Hollies and Freddie & The Dreamers, Merseyside, the undisputed nerve centre of the beat boom threw up Gerry & The Pacemakers, Billy J. Kramer & The Dakotas, and The Merseybeats among others, while way down south in London town, outfits such as Brian Poole & The Tremeloes, The Dave Clark 5, and former Crawdaddy Club favourites, The Rolling Stones, began to break through.

It seemed that wherever you looked bands were springing up, and the sleepy market town of Hereford was no exception. It was here that Peter Overend Watts (born 13th of May, 1947) and Terence Dale Griffin (born 24th of October, 1948) first bumped into each other in the corridors of Ross-on-Wye Grammar School during the autumn of 1963. Watts, Birmingham born, but late of Worthing in Sussex, possessed a Hofner Colorama guitar and fancied himself as a bit of a Brian Jones, while local lad Griffin had recently acquired a small, but by '63 standards, suitably impressive drumkit. Watts had been trying in vain to get a group together, but the stumbling block had always been the chronic shortage of decent drummers at the school. So when he spotted Griffin's kit he wasted no time in offering him the tub-thumping spot in a beat combo he had recently formed called The Anchors. The band's first line up consisted of Watts and Griffin, plus Bob 'Yobbo'

Davies on rhythm guitar and vocals, John 'Grutton' Sutton on double bass, and vocalist Pat O'Donnell. The group never managed to escape the confines of the school, and as summer turned to autumn they lost Davies (now a headmaster) and O'Donnell (today a college lecturer), to be replaced by Paul 'Frizz' Jeffrey on guitar and Robert 'Fishpole' Fisher on lead vocals.

After Christmas, John Sutton departed and for a while the group operated without a bassist, although the recruitment of vocalist Patrick Brooke heralded a switch to bass for second choice singer Fisher. The band operated as The Anchors for a few more months before changing their name to the more demonic sounding Wild Dogs Hellhounds. Lead guitarist Peter Watts remembered that "all we ever used to play was school dances and Conservative Club parties. We were really wild. I had a gold lamé waistcoat made out of curtain material and we used to wear Marks & Spencer see-through shirts with string vests borrowed from our fathers underneath . . . and Beatle wigs! We used to leap about on the stage. Very wild."

Their set list would vary dramatically according to audience whims, although wherever possible the group preferred to shun the current crop of chart fodder (remember, these were still the days when middle of the road performers like Dora Bryan could tear up the Top 20 with such everlasting classics as *All I Want For Christmas Is A Beatle*) for a stroll through more raunchier pastures. "We used to play R&B," remembered Watts. "Everybody would request *24 Hours From Tulsa* and we'd give them *Lucille* and things like that. Pretty horribly as well, I expect. The school hall we used to play in had a trap door in the stage which I would put a rubber bone in before the start. The band would come on and start playing and then I would come on on my own like the big star. I'd drink water out of a bowl with DOG written on the side, then pull up the trap door, take the bone out and chew it. And then I'd pick up the guitar and start playing. The headmaster didn't like us very much."

By the summer of '64, Jeffrey had decided to throw in the towel, forcing the group to carry on as a four piece, somewhat in the style of the then just starting to happen Who. By now Watts had left school and was attempting to seek gainful employment as a trainee architect, although he still harboured pop star ambitions. Deciding that Wild Dogs Hellhounds was maybe a little too satanic for audiences made up mainly of teenagers, the group opted for another change of identity, this time to the more groovy sounding The Soulents. This move proved to be a smart one as increased gigging prompted them to turn semi-pro and even got them a fan club, although the high point of their career turned out to be nothing greater than a second place spot behind Pershore's then finest all girl group, The Ravons, in the final of the Malvern Winter Gardens Beat Contest. Even so, Watts was now well and truly bitten by the beat bug, much to the detriment of his more legitimate occupation. "I worked as a trainee architect, and each night after work I went out to see The Yardbirds or The Who or simply to play myself. At work I constantly fell asleep with my head on the drawing board. Nobody seemed to mind, but they kept telling me to get my hair cut!"

Ever conscious of changing trends, the band had by now broadened their repertoire to include some of the early West Coast psychedelic sounds drifting in over the pirate airwaves from San Francisco. Drummer Griffin remembered that "when we first started out it was like *Clockwork Orange*. We were playing flower power to all the local heavies who were beating the hell out of each other. Their idea of a night out was to come home covered in blood with a few teeth missing!"

It was Griffin, who from the comparative safety of his drumkit, had started to notice "two threatening looking 'teddy boy' types who often stood glaring at us as we played." The heavies in question turned out to be Terry Allen and his cousin John. Terence Allen (born 26th of May, 1944) was originally from the small South Wales mining village of Crynant and had moved with his parents to Hereford in 1960. Griffin later found out that "he and his cousin John would come on a dual mission to (a) look at us playing and (b) to romance the

**Opposite page: Terry "Verden" Allen (photo by Barry Plummer)**

Turner sisters from Tudorville, a tough area of town. It wasn't until some years later that Watts and I found out that he and John came to pick up hints and not to size us up for a beating."

In 1964, Allen had even gone as far as purchasing, via the miracle of h.p., a Vox Continental organ (as recently popularised by Alan Price on *House Of The Rising Sun*) and had joined Hereford combo, The Inmates. The band proved a big hit on the Hereford / Welsh border scene, and their packed diary meant it would be some years before Allen would bump into Watts and Griffin again.

Meanwhile across town, another band formed in that heady summer of '64 were beginning to make a name for themselves. Guitarist Michael Geoffrey Ralphs (born 31st of May, 1944) and his mate Stanley Abdul Tippins (vocals), along with Cyril Townsend on bass plus (à la Spinal Tap), and an alarming succession of drummers, made up The Buddies who turned pro in 1965. They had signed up with London agent, Guy Williams, who had wasted no time in shipping the group off to the Continent for a month. Upon their return, Townsend, deciding that the rigours of five shows a night, greasy food and floors for beds was not the life for him, quit on the eve of the group's second European excursion. Needing a competent bassist in a hurry, Ralphs and Tippins, both from nearby Sarnesfield and Bromyard respectively and therefore familiar with the local scene, finally found their boy languishing in the ranks of the mean and moody The Silence. The plucker in question was none other than Peter Watts, and The Silence were none other than The Soulents one more name change down the line, now opting to adopt a moniker first suggested by their bass player around the time of The Anchors.

Unbeknown to Watts, there was an outfit in London using the same name at that time. Formed in Leatherhead in 1964 as The Chocolate Onions, they changed their name to The Silence in '65, although lack of success prompted another name change, this time to John's Children, along with the recruitment of a cocky young guitarist called Marc Bolan. The band released a couple of records, but failed to do much, although their guitarist later went on to bigger and better things.

Watts had little or no reservations about quitting his day job, believing the European experience would do him the power of good. "I thought, I'll play anything to get out of this shit. So I joined on bass and we went to Germany and Italy . . . and perished." Indeed, it was during his all too brief sojourn with The Buddies that the group taped four songs, of which two, The Coasters' classic, *Young Blood*, plus *Something You Got* were touted by the local press as being due for imminent release on an unknown German label, although history shows the 45 as never seeing the light of day.

Still smacking the sticks was the ever present Terry Griffin, who remembered The Silence playing "a lot of Who material. We played a gig with them in Cheltenham and used their equipment. Watts and Robert Fisher blew up the guitar / bass amp. Moon's kit was the loudest I ever played - he came and glared at me for a while! After the gig, Fishpool sat on the neck of Townsend's Rickenbacker and it broke. We ran away in fear of our lives."

The defection of Watts from their ranks caused the inevitable rift in the band, with Fisher and Brooke opting to stay with the bright lights of The Reeperbahn as members of another Hereford band, The Uncertain Kind. This left Griffin, now somewhat surplus to requirements, kicking his heels back home in Blighty, although as Johnny Smack he kept his hand in, playing sessions for Charles and Kingsley Ward at their aptly named Future Sound Studio. The brothers had previously worked with production wizard Joe Meek as both The Thunderbolts and The Charles Kingsley Creation before drifting into production themselves. For £5 a time Griffin drummed on records by The Interns (*Is It Really What You Want* b/w *Just Like Me*), The Cheatin' Hearts (*Zip Tease* b/w *Bad Kind*) and Yemm & Yemen (*Black Is The Night* b/w *Do Blondes Really Have More Fun?*), all of which were released in 1966.

Returning home from their second Continental crossing, The Buddies found it something of a struggle to get a toehold in a Hereford scene now literally saturated with bands. As was often the case in those early days they believed the answer to the problem was a name change, this time to the tougher sounding The Problem, in the hope that a new identity would herald instant employment. This proved not to be the case, although a gig at a Midlands working men's club afforded a chance meeting with future Traffic guitarist, Dave Mason, recently departed from Brummie band The Hellions, and now scratching a living as a hack musician for visiting solo singers who relied on local pick-up bands for their backing. Mason liked the sound The Problem were making, but felt that their repertoire, which now consisted almost entirely of soul covers, deserved a funkier sounding name. Quick as a flash he suggested The Doc Thomas Group.

So it was, that while Ramsey's raiders were winning the World Cup in the summer of '66, the newly christened Doc Thomas Group were on a ferry to Italy with the prospect of a month's worth of club dates ahead. Italy, then as now, was not noted for its glittering array of blistering R&B and soul acts, and consequently this chronic shortage of home grown talent ensured that the band went down a storm. Their unexpected (to them at least) popularity even resulted in a couple of TV slots and the offer of a recording contract, even if it was with the totally unknown (outside of Italy, that is) Dischi Interrecord. And so that October, the band trudged to Turin to record what was essentially their stage act, under the watchful eye of producer Gian Stellari, the results being issued the following February as the single, *Just Can't Go To Sleep* b/w *Harlem Shuffle,* and the album, *The Doc Thomas Group.* At the time of taping, the band consisted of Stan Tippins (vocals), Mick Ralphs (lead guitar), Pete Watts (bass), Dave Tedstone (rhythm guitar) and Bob Hall (drums), but by the time they got back to Hereford they were subject to yet another in a seemingly endless string of line-up shuffles. Out went Hall to a 9 to 5 job and Tedstone temporarily joined blues rockers, Savoy Brown before fading permanently into obscurity, and in came organist Geoff Lowrey and, from the ranks of the unemployed, drummer Terry Griffin who, although over the moon to be working, remembered literally starving "through not being paid, always coming back completely broke, pushing the van off the Ferry at Dover 'cos there was no petrol left in it."

The band gigged on and off in Italy for the rest of 1967 where they proved remarkably successful, playing regularly at The Bat Caverna Club in Riccione, although they were actually based at the Milano Marittime in Milan. Terry Griffin recalled that "in Milano Marittime we played The Pepper Club in the afternoon, The Pinete in the evening and, on the odd occasion, free spots in an outdoor cafe too, to keep the owners happy. Those were the days! The Doc Thomas Group would do 45-60 minute sets."

In 1973, in an interview with Dick Tatham for *Diana* magazine, Griffin told a story of an experience out in Riccione. It is printed here in full:

*"Around the time the van blew up, we had a string of gigs booked up - some a long way from Riccione. How were we going to get to them without a van?"*

*Romeo was a cab driver the boys knew in Riccione - and they took their problem of getting gigs to him. The gear was in a yellow trailer with ORCHESTRA in red on either side. A bit of hard bargaining led to Romeo agreeing to take them to gigs with the trailer lashed behind his taxi.*

*"To save money, we were all living in one grotty hotel room. Day after day we sat and puzzled over how we were ever going to get home to dear old Britain. Going by plane or train was out, because of all our gear. We just didn't have the money. One day we mentioned our problem to Romeo. He said, 'I take you'. We all said, 'Eh?' Romeo persisted. He said he'd always wanted to go to Britain and would drive us there - trailer and all. He added he'd have to work out the price. Next day he quoted us the equivalent of £180. We did a deal fast."*

*Leave at dawn . . . that was the arrangement. Buffin remembers it was still dark when they heard Romeo drive up. They were all packed and ready and started going down with their luggage. Although Pete was staying on they knew they would have very little room. A slight shock awaited them . . . "I figured we'd just about cope. So imagine our panic when we saw - in the half light - a very large lady sitting next to Romeo."*

*"My wife!" he explained with a grin. "She like treep to England too."*

15

*"That wasn't all. In the back were supplies for Romeo and wife. Two huge containers of red wine, packets of cheese and butter, assorted fruit and so on. Mick, Stan and Verden clambered in with the nosh. I squeezed in front next to Mrs. Romeo."*

Buffin remembers they all changed seats from time to time. All except Mr and Mrs Romeo that is. He didn't want anybody else to drive and she wanted to be next to him.

*"Romeo had estimated the journey at three days (How wrong could anyone be?). After about 250 miles we reached the outskirts of Milan. Romeo lost his way. He said he'd never driven that far before.*

*"About halfway across France a lorry thundering past caught the top of the cab, and sent drums, which had been tied there, scattering along the motorway. We stopped and dashed after them as heavy rain sloshed onto us - luckily they weren't much damaged.*

*"Then, after we'd pulled in for a meal, Romeo discovered he'd lost his keys - a huge bunch of them. Luckily he had a spare ignition key so we could press on. At last we chugged on to the Channel ferry. When we reached Dover the customs asked us to unlock the trailer. We said we'd lost our keys, but their reply was a sarcastic laugh and, 'We seem to have heard that one before'. So we had to smash the trailer open, just to make sure we weren't smuggling anything into the country."*

The group gigged on and off in Italy for the remainder of 1967, their blend of hard edged R&B and stompin' soul covers continued to prove successful, although poor sales of their records (they were essentially known as a club act) plus unscrupulous promoters conspired to keep the band broke and hungry. Their popularity was reflected in the fact that the locals idolised Stan Tippins, going as far as to dub him "The Sinatra Of Beat", although in fairness, their only serious competition in the Latin sweepstakes was a group called The Casuals, former three times winners of TV's *Opportunity Knocks* in the early Sixties, who reputedly regularly whipped the locals into a frenzy in the bars of downtown Milan.

While far from adverse to the ecstatic applause of Italian audiences, The Doc Thomas Group began to get restless, sensing their soul boy image was turning into something of a straightjacket. Mick Ralphs told *ZigZag* magazine some years later that "the gigs in Italy lasted, on and off, for a couple of years and gave us a good deal of experience. Good English groups were very popular over there at the time, but we really got sick of pandering to the pop crowd. We really wanted to play our own music."

Dissent over direction led to the defection of Lowrey (he would later turn up as organist with German progressive rock combo Lake) and he was replaced by another Hereford boy, Terry Allen, who was now working intermittently with a local musical collective known as The Shakedown Sound, who were essentially a loose band of musicians who came and went as whims (and finances) dictated. Allen had got the gig on the strength of his ownership of a Hammond C3 organ and Leslie Tone cabinet, a real coup for a musician back in the days when even headline acts borrowed each others amps and fed their sound through a house p.a. which invariably doubled as the bingo callers sound system. The mighty Hammond (for it truly was the giant of its gender) had been invented by one Laurence Hammond, something of an all round genius who had also developed automatic transmission for cars in 1909, a non-ticking clock, a process for refining sugar and a primitive 3-D film system. Not being a man to rest on his laurels, he had debuted his keyboard invention in 1939, and its numerous switches and bass pedals had given it that trademarked 'heavy' sound. It initially found favour with jazz acts in the late Fifties (remember The Peddlers?), but it was R&B pioneer Graham Bond who, in March 1963, first hit on the idea of feeding the C3 through a Leslie speaker cabinet, in the process producing a deep rasping sound previously unheard. Although the idea was considered extremely innovative, very few bands picked up on it, so for Terry Allen, stuck out in the backwaters of the Welsh borders, to own a C3 with a Leslie cabinet was, apart from being considered terribly radical, something of an open invitation to join any of the new breed of progressive bands looking to beef up their sound.

So it was that, after a brief spell working in a garage after quitting The Inmates, Allen, with keyboard, was invited to join The Shakedown Sound in late '67. The band found work backing Jimmy Cliff, still languishing in his pre-reggae soul man days, and Allen played on Cliff's Island single, *Hard Road To Travel*, along with Mick Ralphs, who was in the band at the time on one of his soon to be regular on-off stints. It was Ralphs, discontented with the 'pop' stance of The Docs, who had first toyed with the notion of joining the ranks of Beach Boys copycats, Tony Rivers & The Castaways, before finally seeing sense and opting to join The Shakedown Sound. In turn, this prompted the equally frustrated Griffin, on hearing that Mick Fleetwood had quit as drummer for John Mayall's Bluesbreakers, to audition for the vacant stool. The history books record that he lost out to Keef Hartley but, undeterred, he auditioned for Love Sculpture (Dave Edmunds and John David Williams) at Rockfield. "I remember doing *A Day In The Life* and *River Deep Mountain High*. Having played, Edmunds offered me the job, but I said I would have to think about it. He was not pleased. When I was about to leave I found my car battery flat (it was a rather beat up Vauxhall Victor saloon), and Edmunds and John David refused to push it."

With Ralphs and Allen away backing Jimmy Cliff, the remainder of The Docs decided to audition for a new guitarist, although the only half decent applicant was a young punk by the name of Les Tuckey who, deciding that a future with a second division soul band was not his style, opted to wait for something better to come along. He was rewarded a couple of years later when he landed a gig backing Detroit rocker Suzi Quatro, a partnership that continued to the altar and beyond. At this time the group were signed to an agency in Swansea called Vee-Jay (no relation to the U.S. label of the same name), a relationship which, while proving less than fruitful financially, resulted in more than the odd gig in South Wales. South Wales though was hardly the nerve centre of the music biz - Griffin remembered around this time being "involved in a very nasty incident at a gig near Ross-On-Wye in which Stan and Verden were forced to punch out several very violent guys in the audience. A riot ensued and the police were called. They advised us to use cymbals as weapons to throw discus-style at troublemakers!").

In an attempt to widen their audience base, Griffin, Watts and Tippins decided, upon the return to the fold of Ralphs and Allen, to take up the mantle of The Shakedown Sound. The thinking behind this move was that the name was well known to club-goers in the West Midlands (something of a happening area at the time) who had seen Jimmy Cliff. As no one actually owned the name, The Doc Thomas Group simply stole it, although not before they were forced to perform a short stint backing former Jimmy Cliff bassist, Johnny Lee, as

TALBOT CLUB
presents
DANCE
to the Explosive
SHAKEDOWN
SOUND
at
THE TALBOT HOTEL
KNIGHTWICK
Friday, 19th April
*Licensed Bar applied for*
9.30 p.m. to 1.30 a.m.
Admission 6/-

Lee Starr & The Astrals, an outfit which also featured their former guitarist Dave Tedstone.

The change of name to The Shakedown Sound failed to pay the expected dividends and by the Autumn of '68 the band were back in Hereford billing themselves as The Silence, gigging here and there with one eye always fixed firmly on the wants ads. It was a response to one such ad in *Melody Maker* that resulted in Ralphs and Watts travelling to London to audition for a new band called Free. As usual they didn't get the gig, but drummer Griffin remembered that "at the rehearsal room they met Paul Rodgers, Simon Kirke and a hyperactive pipecleaner of a figure, their record producer, Guy Stevens. He was much given to violent nodding of his head when the group were playing, and if it got really steaming his foot would stomp exaggeratedly. Paul and Simon had this same quirk. Ralphs and Watts noted this for possible future reference."

Watts also recalled the audition, saying that "I noticed that Simon Kirke and Paul Rodgers were raving, shaking their heads a lot, and Guy was getting into it, shaking his head".

With the vacancies in Free finally going to Paul Kossoff and Andy Fraser, it was back to the classifieds for The Silence. A couple of leads came their way, but they ended up failing auditions to back two all girl groups from Sweden, The Paper Dolls and The Pearlettes, as well as being turned down by Macca and his chums over at Apple, where, in reference to their rural roots, they were dubbed "The Archers".

As a last resort, Griffin contacted his old mate Kingsley Ward at Rockfield Studios in Monmouthshire and talked him into taping a 4-track demo. The group recorded *The Rebel* (a Ward song recently popularised by Love Sculpture on the BBC's *Top Gear* show), *Find Your Way* by Ralphs, Pete Watts' *The Wreck*, and a Ralphs inspired instrumental called *The Silence*. Deciding to limit the tape to three tracks, they promptly ditched *The Wreck*, had a whip round for petrol money, and sent Ralphs off to London.

Remembering the recent failed Free audition, the guitarist headed straight for Island Records and the office of Guy Stevens. Figuring a large helping of bullshit was in order, he barged right in and threw the tapes on the producers desk, immediately getting the required reaction. "He was so taken aback that he asked me to sit down, and we ended up coming to London for an audition."

Stevens, at the time just out of jail and still looking for a band to fit the name he had urged his wife to keep a secret, told the *NME* that "I knew they had to be right, have the right attitude. Then I saw these blokes lugging an organ up the stairs, and they were really LUGGING this fucking great organ up the stairs. It was enormous, a Hammond C3 the size of a piano, and I thought, 'I don't care what they sound like. They've done it. They got the organ up the stairs'."

In fact it was seven days later when the lugging of the organ actually took place (the location was the tiny Spot Studio in South Molton Street), but having done so, The Silence performed a set consisting of *Wide Asleep* (Ralphs), *Mystic Balls* (Watts), *Another Country* (The Electric Flag), *Northern Hemisphere* (East Of Eden) and Kingsley Ward's *The Rebel*. As per the Free audition, Watts "mentioned to Mick that he ought to shake his head a lot - and we all shook our heads like mad - and he (Stevens) was shaking his. I thought, 'This is it.' We were great!"

Terry Griffin also recalled that "On the day we all nodded our heads furiously and stamped our feet as we played. Guy began to do so too. He liked us."

Like them he did, except for one band member. "Guy loved the band, but he wanted us to get a new singer," said Ralphs. "He felt Stan didn't look right."

Surprisingly, for one who had had more than his share of false dawns in the past, Tippins took the rejection gracefully, and within weeks went back to Italy to resume his career as "The Sinatra Of Beat". Within a year he would be back, but this time as a road manager. Right now the band needed a replacement. The hunt was on for a front man.

*"Island Records Ltd needs pianist / singer to join exciting hard rock band playing Bob Dylan influenced country rock music. Immediate album recording work. Ring REGENT 6225."*
*GUY STEVENS - MELODY MAKER WANT AD.*

*"When I started all you needed was a Vox AC30 and a Framus Star bass and you were nearly there."*
*IAN HUNTER.*

**CHAPTER**

# 3

Ian Patterson had always fancied himself as a bit of a rebel. Born Ian Hunter Patterson on the 3rd of June, 1939, in Oswestry, Shropshire, the only son of a policeman, he grew up in Dundee before his father moved the family back south to Shrewsbury. Here, young Ian, who always resented the authoritarian figure his father presented and the jibes from schoolmates that came from being the offspring of a copper, blossomed into a textbook Fifties juvenile delinquent - into girls, bikes, D.A.s and, most importantly of all, Jerry Lee Lewis. "I thought I was ill," he was later to say in an interview for Capital Radio. "In fact my parents were talking about having me committed at one time. And that was only because I couldn't mix."

It was being knocked back by a young maiden of tender years by the name of Irene Wilde at Barker Street bus station that spurred him on to take up writing songs in his mother's living room, fuelling his burning ambition to "be somebody someday". Hunter later recounted this story in a song, admitting that "it's the truth. Irene really snubbed me at the bus station and inspired me to be a star. She's still there, married and enormous, of course, but I meant what I wrote in that song."

Leaving school at the earliest possible opportunity (in those days 15 years of age), he commenced punching in for work, doing dead end jobs in the town's numerous factories, although his speciality in those days was either as a fitter or grinder. Always an avid rock'n'roll fan, he had harboured an ambition to play in a group since his early teens and, following a brief but uneventful stint as a trainee journalist for the *Wellington Evening Journal* and *The Shrewsbury News*, he began practising guitar in earnest.

In 1961, following a move to Northampton, he was competent enough to pick up the odd gig on the local scene, especially as he was more than willing to have a go at playing bass, although he was later honest enough to admit that in those early days, "I couldn't play properly. I was just in love with the idea of show business."

Things took a turn for the better when Patterson heard the first strangled warblings of a folkie from New York, and it was Bob Dylan who really gave him the kick up the backside he needed. "I worked day jobs . . . I had over 40 jobs. It was the time when the only singer was Cliff Richard, and I thought I could never sing like that, let alone get paid and earn my living from being a musician. Then Bob Dylan came along and changed things. Before that I'd just watched Cliff on TV and felt helpless."

In classic bad boy style, Patterson had endured a shotgun wedding and by 1964 he was married with two kids (Stephen and Tracie). The love of showbusiness outweighed any family considerations though, and that year saw the newly converted Dylan disciple playing in an outfit called The Homelanders who operated mainly in the Nottingham area. It was while working in the Midlands that he met pianist Freddie "Fingers" Lee, who at the time was a member of The Savages, Screaming Lord Sutch's backing band. Lee liked the young guitarist and, following a quiet word in the ear of his boss, Patterson was taken on board, although he was forced to play bass due to the recent recruitment of a flashy young guitarist named Richie Blackmore.

**Opposite page: Ian Hunter (photo by Barry Plummer)**

Sutch was a star in Hamburg, the second home of a brace of British bands back then, and The Savages were soon treading the boards at the city's famous Star Club. For Patterson it was a dream come true, especially since his last legitimate job had been digging holes in the road for Northampton District Council. He later admitted though that "I never made any money. The little I got I spent on food and drink. Half the time they wouldn't pay you at all. The clubs usually booked bands for the whole evening; our first show was at five in the afternoon - our last ended at five in the morning. I remember one show in Rendsburg. We played nine hours non stop."

After a suitably backbreaking stint with Sutch, Patterson formed his own combo to tread the Reeperbahn boards under the handle of Hurricane Henry & The Shriekers. As well as backing Freddie "Fingers " Lee (as Freddie Lee & The Shriekers), they played many a gig in their own right. Their leader recalled that "the band went down a storm everywhere we played. There was one problem though. We didn't get paid. The inevitable happened; we were stranded on the docks without our fares home, and if it hadn't been for the sympathy of various frauliens we probably wouldn't have got back."

It soon dawned on Patterson that he was trapped in a musical treadmill, nothing more than a rock'n'roll commuter, journeying between factory life in Northampton, night clubs in Hamburg and U.S. airforce bases in Kiel. "I used to get very depressed at the time. Sometimes for six weeks or longer. You go to Germany, work, get ripped off, come back to do six to eight weeks of regular jobs until you get the next gig."

It was during one of these enforced stays back home that he landed a gig playing bass for the totally unknown Apex Rhythm & Blues All Stars, who taped four songs which were released by the local "you pay we press" outfit, John Lever Records, situated at 52 Gold Street, Northampton. The EP, which featured the standards *Tall Girl*, *Reelin' And Rockin'*, *Down The Road Apiece*, and *Sugar Shack*, had a run of 500 copies - marginally less than *The Friendly Undertaker* b/w *Little Bit More* single that Fontana issued, featuring the vocal talents of Freddie Lee plus the erstwhile bassist in his role as a Shrieker. Neither disc was destined to set the world alight.

Undeterred, Lee used the same band on two further Fontana singles, Boyce & Hart's *I'm Gonna Buy Me A Dog* b/w *I Can't Drive*, and *Bossy Boss* b/w *Don't Run Away*, the latter being credited to Fingers Lee & The Upper Hand.

By the Spring of '67, Patterson had moved his wife and kids out from the sticks and into a cramped bedsit in London's Archway, and had joined guitarist Miller Anderson in a band called The Scenery. Money was still so tight that he was forced to work day shifts as a capstan operator and occasional van driver, even though he didn't have a driving licence.

Rather suddenly that summer, and on the recommendation of Lee, Patterson along with a young organist from the Hamburg scene called Roger Glover, whose band Episode 6 had just suffered the indignity of playing army bases in the Lebanon for two months, landed a job as a songwriter for publishers Francis Day & Hunter and their offshoot Peer Music for the princely sum of £15 a week. Patterson proved particularly unprolific, although Freddie & The Dreamers, long past their sell-by date, recorded *Gilbert The Ghost*, Louisiana Jane White taped *Seasons Song* and Dave Berry used *When I Have Learned To Dream* as the flipside of his *Forever* 45. Eventually, the budding Bacharach was forced to concede that "I was getting a bit embarrassed 'cos they weren't using much of my stuff. The lyrics were schmaltzy . . . real middle of the road stuff."

In January, 1968, Patterson and Anderson teamed up with Lee and drummer Pete Philips to form At Last The 1958 Rock'n'Roll Show, and in March CBS issued a single, *I Can't Drive* b/w *Working On The Railroad*. The disc was even allocated a tiny promotion budget which resulted in a feature in the 9th of March issue of *Melody Maker*, where the band's bass player explained to the newspaper's readers that "we've retained the earthy spirit of rock to get a fuller sound, because rhythm sections are so much better today" (sure Ian, go tell that to the boys at Sun Studios). Despite (or maybe because of) Patterson's comments, the record stiffed, even although no less a luminary than Tom Jones later had a crack at recording the A-side (he rather wisely opted to bury it as an album track however).

Undeterred, the band promptly changed their name to Charlie Woolfe and released a version of the old Carter-Lewis / Geoff Stevens stomper, *Dance Dance Dance*, coupled with the Cheeseman (Freddie's real name) / Anderson / Patterson composition, *Home*. The platter was produced by veteran knob twiddler, Jimmy Duncan, and was issued by the NEMS label, although once again the world conspired to look the other way.

And so it was that the summer of '68 saw Patterson hustling for a gig with The New Yardbirds, only to lose out to John Paul Jones, a session buddy of band leader Jimmy Page, who then decided that a change of name to Led Zeppelin was in order. Now dropped by Francis Day & Hunter, Patterson managed to find work with Leeds Music, although a commission to pen tunes for Englebert Humperdink, the heart-throb of the blue rinse brigade, turned out to be something of a non-starter, with the frustrated bard finally acknowledging that "they weren't getting anything out of me except tax relief."

By the following summer, Patterson, in an effort to forge something of a new identity, had taken to calling himself Hunter, although the switch seemed to have little effect - he was still stuck in a rut working day jobs in factories and hustling for the odd gig at weekends. In an effort to aid future auditions, he decided to tape a few songs. "At the time I was making demos at Bill Farleys in Denmark Street. He had a little 4-track studio and he'd only charge four quid an hour - Jimi Hendrix, The Stones and The Who had all been in there. I sang in this odd Dylany voice, 'cos I couldn't sing properly. Anyway, Bill rang me up and said, 'You gotta come down and see this band. They've been trying people out and don't like anyone. But they're weird so they might like you'."

*"About 12 people turned up and were terrible. All of them. Ian
was dreadful but he was the best of a terrible lot. Guy said we
ought to take him on just to show Island that we'd got someone
- if only for a couple of weeks."*

*PETE WATTS.*

*"I knew I was going to be the
front man. They probably didn't
realise it, but I did. I'd been
waiting for that all my life."*

*IAN HUNTER.*

**CHAPTER**

# 4

On the 5th of June, 1969, Ian Hunter was taken on as pianist / singer with the recently re-christened Silence. After much cajoling on the part of Guy Stevens, they had reluctantly agreed to call themselves Mott The Hoople, but only after turning down Griff Fender and Savage, Rose & Fixable, two of the maverick producer's other suggestions. Organist Allen thought their new name "sounded like a racehorse", while Hunter, having browsed through Stevens' dog-eared prison pilfered copy of the Manus novel based around a character called Norman Mott, believed that "it's about an eccentric guy who didn't fit in anywhere and ended up in a circus of freaks. Finally he got in a hot air balloon and dumped the sandbags. He was last seen three miles from heaven." Little did he know at the time, but his own story would follow a remarkably similar line. Initially, Hunter was somewhat sceptical of both the band and Stevens. He recalled that "they never said a word; it was real odd. I knew Pete Watts was worried because he didn't think I looked right. The others said they liked me, but they were really shy people."

Guy Stevens, in an interview some years later with journalist Charles Shaar Murray, threw some light on the band's initial encounter with their new boy. "Lemme tell you about Hunter. The first time . . . changing buses twice to get to what he thought was some dodgy demo session. He didn't know what it was going to be. The guy at Regent Sound just told him that there was some bloke rambling on about Jerry Lee Lewis and Bob Dylan."

After turning up at the tiny studio, the new recruit conceded that his appearance may have been a little off putting, particularly as at the time he was "fat, had short hair and wore stupid clothes because I had no money. Now when you have no money, you can still get decent stuff, but back then cheap clothes were terrible. I did have my shades though."

Guitarist Ralphs thought the cheap sunglasses looked positively tacky. "I didn't think Ian intended to keep wearing his shades, but Guy told him he should never take them off. Ian tried to rebel against that, but everyone kept telling him to put the shades back on."

Drummer Griffin also had vivid memories of that initial meeting with Hunter. "He wore open toed sandals, a wretched donkey jacket, and his hair, which was red and curly, tried without success to be long. Plus he sported big black shades. He was 'basically a bass player' and snatched up a bass to demonstrate. It was fast, flummoxing and futile. The stick insect coaxed 'young ginger' onto the piano stool, and it was agreed that he would bash out a song called *Like A Rolling Stone*. At the curtailment of this musical event the stick insect leapt, foamed at the mouth, burbled and raved goggle-eyed in an orgasmic outflow of triumph, delight and relief. Guy Stevens had found his man."

Another member of the band totally bemused by the proceedings was bassist Pete Watts, who remembered that "Ian sat down at the piano and sang *Like A Rolling Stone*. At least he had an idea. He wasn't a good piano player and he wasn't a good singer, but there was something about him. So we decided to take him for a couple of weeks and see what happened."

**Above: Mott The Hoople (photo courtesy of Island)**

No one was more amazed by the whole deal than Hunter, who many years later admitted that "Guy Stevens was very, very special, because if it hadn't been for him seeing that glimmer of whatever that I certainly wasn't aware of, I'd still be working in the factory right now."

The audition certainly appeared to be something of a last ditch affair for the would be singer. Years of bumming around on the semi-pro circuit with all of its financial uncertainties had left him bitter and broke, and trapped in a crumbling marriage with no future. He was looking for an escape hatch, and when Guy Stevens gave him the nod, he was in like a shot, and within 24 hours his appointment was made official. "The next day I had a letter from Island Records confirming it. My influence was Sonny Bono more than Dylan (Hunter had also attempted Bono's *Laugh At Me* during the audition, but it was something of a non-starter) though I wasn't impressed by either one at the time. I joined the group because it was £15 a week at the time and I was skint."

*"I went in and got the gig and started this strange relationship. It was really funny 'cos half the time I thought they were lousy and half the time I thought they were ten times better than I could ever be."*

*"It was really funny. He was in the group but we never saw him. He lived in the Archway with his wife and we all lived in a flat in Chelsea."*

*PETE WATTS.*

**CHAPTER**

**5**

**Having finally found the missing piece to his musical jigsaw puzzle, Guy Stevens wasted no time in getting the band down on tape, even although they had little in the way of recordable material worked up. The producer booked The Pied Bull, an old pub which had recently acquired a degree of hipness due to the patronage of Graham Bond who, after the break up of his band The Organisation, had played sessions in the large upstairs room with various local musicians, including Peter Frampton on guitar and music journalist Chris Welch on drums. Pete Watts remembered the whole thing as a blur. "We had rehearsals booked at The Pied Bull pub in Islington. This was in June, 1969. I think *Half Moon Bay* came out of it - it was really the band playing *At The Crossroads* backwards - so we thought it wasn't so bad after all. We did the album which seemed pretty good. It was all done in a week. Guy was producing it, it was real wild. We then went back to rehearsals - subsequent live gigs were pretty bad and it was so boring. Only Ian would turn up in the morning, the rest of us used to arrive at two or three in the afternoon. We didn't realise the significance of what was going on, the record deal and all that. Poor old Ian. He's really putting a lot into it and we didn't care."**

Guy Stevens had booked a week in July at Morgan Studios on Willesden High Road because (a) it was cheap and (b) it sported a large well stocked downstairs bar. The band shuffled in and were fed vast quantities of alcohol by their producer, who then commanded them to plug in and play, with the subsequent results surrepticiously taped by engineer Andy Johns. Organist Allen remembered that the sessions were "on 8-track , and when we went in and did it there was none of this messing about and overdubbing. We had one track each and that was it."

Bearing in mind the band had only recently ditched their soul boy image for a more progressive stance and had, for a lead singer, a new member who confessed to being unable to sing in the accepted fashion and who worked from a song book consisting of two tunes, the results of their first rehearsals were remarkably self assured, if a little rough around the edges. They recorded 17 songs at Morgan Studios, with eight making it to the album, although one number, the Hunter penned *Road To Birmingham*, would be the subject of some dispute. The tune had been taped towards the end of the week and featured Ralphs on bass due to Watts being absent because of illness, but Hunter later complained that "on our first album a number called *The Road To Birmingham* was put on the album instead of *Rock'n'Roll Queen*. We didn't even know about it until after the release. They changed it after the first 5,000 copies."

In fact, both *Road To Birmingham* and *Rock'n'Roll Queen* appeared on the first pressing of the album, although the former was subsequently substituted for *Backsliding Fearlessly*. To add to the confusion, *Backsliding Fearlessly* was always listed on the cover and label - whether it appeared or not! Consequently, copies of that initial run of albums on the pink Island label now change hands for upwards of £30 at record fairs. That original batch of 5,000 also included slightly different mixes of *Laugh At Me* and *Wrath & Roll*.

Included among the songs that didn't make the final cut were The Silence's audition speciality, *The Rebel*, which was recorded twice with Ralphs and Hunter both having a crack at vocals, plus Watt's *The Wreck*, Chuck Berry's *Little Queenie*, a Hunter rocker called *Back In The States Again*, and two Dylan classics, *Can You Please Crawl Out Your Window* and *Just Like Tom Thumb Blues*. The latter two were omitted mainly because Hunter's songs at the time sounded like Dylan bootlegs anyway.

Originally titled *Talking Bear Mountain Picnic Massacre Disaster Dylan Blues*, which thankfully remained nothing more than a figment of Guy Stevens' colourful imagination, the album that was initially scheduled for a 5th of October release, finally crawled out in November. Self titled and housed in a gatefold sleeve (positively de rigueur at the time), its cover featured an Escher painting depicting the circle of life, while the inner cover sported a portrait of the band shot outside Island's Basing Street Studios on what appeared to be a very windy morning, causing Allen, who had his hat pinched by Griffin, to complain that "my hair ended up looking like a Ted in that photo."

The band, as well as assuming a new collective identity, had also - with the exception of Ralphs - all undergone personal name changes. Ian Patterson received his first official credit as Hunter, Peter Watts began using his middle name of Overend, while Terence Dale Griffin was credited as Buffin, a nickname he had picked up at the time of The Anchors, the term of endearment being a corruption of the continually flu-bugged Snivillin' Griffin to Snivillin 'Griff Buffin to plain old Buffin. The last band member to undergo a name change courtesy of the errant producer was organist Terry Allen, who remembered "Guy bringing in the sleeve for our first LP and he said, 'Right, we're doing the sleeve right now. Your name. Terence Allen. The name. We can't use that. You've got five minutes to think of one.' So I said, 'Well I can always use my father's name, Verdun with a U. Put an E on instead - Verden Allen.' Guy said, 'Oh yeah, Verden. That's not bad'. Next thing it's on the sleeve."

The album kicked off with a head first deep end instrumental plunge into The Kinks' beat era barnstormer, *You Really Got Me*. Originally sporting something of a lightweight vocal by Ralphs, the track had been transformed into a sub-metal style workout by Stevens, the uncrowned king of compression who simply opened up the faders all the way and slung the vocal track out the window. Interestingly, although it sounds like a natural opener, the song was the last to be recorded, and that was mainly out of desperation. Ian Hunter remembered that "when we first started we were doing slow songs. Anything we did was slow. And Island was getting all upset because we didn't get any reaction when we went out. So Mick Ralphs said 'Let's put this on the end and see what happens'."

Next up was a version of The Sir Douglas Quintet's *At The Crossroads*. Written by band leader Doug Sahm, the song had been featured on their *Mendico album*, something of a cult classic on its release in March, 1969. Hunter warbles through the number in his best *Blonde On Blonde* Dylan-style drone, while the band, led by the cavalry charge of Allen's driving organ, thrash away behind him. Hunter later revealed that *At The Crossroads* "was the first song we were ever known for . . . the first song people actually started clapping before we did the song."

*Laugh At Me* was written in 1965 by Sonny Bono as a sly protest at being denied entry to Martonsi, a popular L.A. music biz watering hole located at 1523 Cahuenga in downtown Hollywood. *I Got You Babe* was on the chart and the boy Bono was hot, although not hot enough it seemed to gain access into the inner sanctum of the eaterie. It has to be said though that the establishment was somewhat old fashioned in its attitude and Bono and his buddy, DJ and local groupie god, Rodney "Mayor Of Sunset Strip" Bingenheimer, were decked out in afghans, faded denims and shoulder length hair (your standard rock star hippy impression at the time). Suitably miffed at being shunned, Sonny boy went home and wrote the song which, when released as a single in September, 1965, reached not only the ears of Ian Hunter, but number nine in the U.K. charts. Vocally, Hunter sticks pretty close to the Bono blueprint, although the song builds dramatically after a slow start, allowing the band to rock out into the fade. Hunter, who obviously saw a similarity between himself and the terminally unhip Bono, said at the time that *Laugh At Me* "was the song I auditioned for Mott with. It was easy to sing. Sonny Bono couldn't sing that well - and I sort of liked people who couldn't sing that well. It was a good song, and people used to laugh at me. I wore shades when it wasn't fashionable to wear them - and I did have a big head. I was extremely arrogant and I kinda liked it that way."

The side closed with Hunter's *Backsliding Fearlessly*, a slow dirge featuring a catchy chorus ("If the world saluted you / What would you do?") plus the singer's soon to be trademarked hamfisted piano, which usually made him sound as if he was playing while wearing a pair of oversized boxing gloves. He sings in his practised Dylan drawl, which comes as no surprise as, on closer inspection, the song turns out to be a rather thinly disguised rewrite of The Zims' *The Times They Are A Changing*.

Side two waded in with Mick Ralphs' good times rave-up, *Rock'n'Roll Queen*, which gave the band their first opportunity to really kick some ass. Featuring a riff not too far removed from The Stones' *Live With Me*, the song kicks up a stink about the good time girls who latch on to rock bands, and with its infectiously hummable chorus ("You're just a Rock'n'Roll Queen / You know what I mean / And I'm just a Rock'n'Roll star"), it was the first of many odes to groupies the group would commit to vinyl over the next few years. Verden

27

Allen remembered that the band were kicking their heels, looking for ideas. "When we were recording we needed one number, a rock thing. And Mick sort of came up with it out of the blue." Once again, necessity proved to be the mother of invention.

*Rabbit Foot And Toby Time*, a Mick Ralphs soft shoed blues-based shuffle was, while being a bit of a toe tapper, nothing more than instrumental candy floss, a sweet sticky filler whose main purpose was to lead the listener gently into the album's big number, the 11 minute DeMille-like epic that was *Half Moon Bay*. It featured the newly patented "'I'm asking a lot of questions, but getting no answers" Hunter lyric over a Ralphs' chord rundown which was essentially *At The Crossroads* in reverse. Verden Allen remembered working on the track, desperately trying to experiment with organ sounds to build up some kind of mood, when Island's head honcho walked through the door on one of his periodic progress checks. "Chris Blackwell had a new girlfriend at the time. When we did that grating organ bit she said, 'What's that sound? I like that. It's fantastic. What's it about?' At a loss as to what Hunter's lyric was actually about, the bemused organist shrugged and replied, 'I haven't got a clue. I don't know'. She said, 'Well it sounds nice anyhow'. So Blackwell says, 'Carry on lads' and walked out."

The album closed with the second piece of filler, the Guy Stevens' "composition", *Wrath & Roll*, which was not actually a song as such, just a random snippet of tape featuring the band joyriding through the closing stages of *Rock'n'Roll Queen* at 100mph before plunging headlong over the ravine into the bottomless pit of the run off groove. This head on collision of instruments mixed straight up front so as to throw the dB meter right into the red, gave the listener a pretty fair indication of what to expect at a Mott live show, as well as providing an insight into a band who, while never shirking from the slow introspective ballads, liked nothing better than a bit of full tilt heads down no nonsense boogie.

While not wishing to take anything away from the band, it was pretty obvious that the sounds emanating from the grooves were the product of Guy Stevens' mangled psyche. Mick Ralphs readily acknowledged that the band were initially nothing more than putty in Stevens' hands when he said that "Guy wanted us to become like Dylan's *Blonde On Blonde* period, and we were so desperate to get ahead that it was fine by us." Buffin backed this up by saying that "Guy Stevens would tell us over and over, 'You are the Rolling Stones, you are Bob Dylan, you are up there with them, you are better than them'. We believed him after a while. There was no alternative."

Always the hustler, Guy Stevens decided that the quickest route to credibility for the band was via the columns of London's then ultra hip underground press. And so it was that the October 10/23 edition of *International Times* carried the first ever interview with the band. To be fair to the (uncredited) journalist, Stevens had slipped him a white label copy of the album with no song titles or biographical information, while the interview with the band came about purely by chance when the writer, calling 'round to chase up Stevens for some record reviews, bumped into the band who, for want of nothing better to do, were hanging out at the producer's pad. Consequently, Hunter is listed as Ian Grant, *Backsliding Fearlessly* is written up as If *The World Saluted You*, while *You Really Got Me* somehow gets mistaken for The Who's *I Can't Explain*! Nevertheless, the article provides a pretty accurate portrait of where the band's heads were at at the time. Hunter acknowledges the Dylan influence, although points out that "to be quiet honest, I never write any song with Dylan consciously in mind", while Mick Ralphs concedes that "I feel everything we write and play is musically valid. I don't think of us as copying anybody, but I should mention that the group in its present form has only been together for about three months, and so our initial writing efforts are, well, affected by our greatest influences. We're still a very new group you see. After we've been together a bit longer I think Mott The Hoople's music will get more involved. We won't lose our influences as such, they'll just be expressed in a different way, perhaps."

Hunter also throws some light onto the mysterious *Road To Birmingham* track, explaining that it was essentially a song about racial prejudice. "The song's about Birmingham, USA, as well as our Birmingham . . . they've got the same problems with their black people. I know it's been said before, but it still hasn't been said enough. I think it's scandalous that we should set up offices in the Commonwealth countries to try and attract people to come here to live, then treat 'em like shit when they get here. I just can't stand racial prejudice and there seems to be a lot of it in the Midlands." Wisely hedging his bets, he added, "I'm not saying that, in certain cases, it's not without cause. I'm just saying that I can't stand it."

The unknown reviewer nailed his flag to the mast by gushing breathlessly that "firstly, Mott The Hoople are a rock'n'roll band. Let there be no mistake about that. They play rugged, almost crude rhythms, and they manage to emanate the almost ecstatic naiveté of the Terry Denes, Johnny Gentles and Grant Thunderers (who?) of the late Fifties. But their nature, the actual basic structures of their numbers, are more complex, more inspired, than those dreadful monstrosities that Tin Pan Alley churned out for so long. They have brought a tenuous (and probably transitory) sophistication to rock'n'roll and in doing so have transcended the acid / progressive rock of the late Sixties and become the only rock'n'roll band of the Seventies currently around."

The man with the pen also found time to climb off his critical hobby horse to get back down to earth and inform his hip and happening readership that "what has been produced in a few months holds incredible promise for the future."

And with that the band were off and running.

As soon as the album was in the can, Guy Stevens whisked his boys over to Italy and to the scene of many a Doc Thomas Group triumph, The Bat Caverna Club, where, commencing on the 6th of August 1969, they played for a fortnight under a cloud of anonymity in preparation for their all important U.K. debut. The two weeks were designed to give the band time to put together a stage show and to try to get to grips with a few songs as well as themselves. From behind his kit, drummer Buffin remembered their debut on Latin soil as being "a remarkable triumph. They loved us even more than we could justify. The next night nothing."

Initially confused, it quickly dawned on the band that the sudden and dramatic turnaround in audience affection was solely down to Hunter's cheap sunglasses. Over to Buffin again. "The first night the audience believed Ian to be blind - and with all the stumbling, fumbling and bad chords, who could blame them? When they realised that our boy was sighted they lost all interest and the Bat management were howling for the return of Stan, the Sinatra of Beat."

*"I was in love with treading the boards. I was fascinated by the stage and the curtains, it wasn't really anything to do with music. I just liked showing off."*

IAN HUNTER.

*"The first gig actually wasn't very good at all. That was with King Crimson. I remember them standing around a white Mellotron. That was something else. Then we did an R.A.F. base next. I think Ian used to sit down and play with a suit on."*
VERDEN ALLEN.

## CHAPTER

# 6

Mott The Hoople made their official U.K. live debut on the 5th of September, 1969, supporting label mates King Crimson at the Market Hall in Romford. Also that month they supported Free in Sunderland prior to making their London debut at the Speakeasy on the 7th of October, and by now they finally had some product to push with the release of the *Rock'n'Roll Queen / Road To Birmingham* 45, which Island had issued at the beginning of the month. The single, while failing to set the charts alight, received the critical thumbs up from the DJs at the hipper end of the market, and resulted in the band being invited to audition (a standard procedure in those days . . . even The Beatles had to do it) for the BBC's *Top Gear* radio show at the Corporation's Maida Vale studios.

The esteemed panel of white coated judges deemed them suitable for exposure on the airwaves, although it would be February of the following year before they were actually invited to record a session. Meanwhile, Island finally got around to releasing the album, which meant that the remainder of the year was spent on the gig trail promoting the plastic.

December was a particularly hectic month, kicking off with the first of what would be many shows at the hippest place in the Home Counties, Aylesbury Friars, a venue started by local promoter Dave Stopps to fill mundane Monday nights at the local ex-servicemen's club. As well as Mott, Genesis and Free were early regulars at the club, culminating in a rapid rise in the popularity stakes and an enforced move to the nearby Borough Assembly Hall. Complaints from the local old soldiers served to hasten matters. The switch to a more spacious abode meant that the club could now accommodate 500 punters as well as its own newsletter, written by a starstruck young student from the local tech called Kris Needs who, at the time, was also one half of a local duo with former classmate and market square weirdo, John Otway. Upon leaving full time education, Needs would join the local *Bucks Advertiser* as a journalist, pen pieces for the daddy of all British fanzines, *Zigzag*, and, in 1972, form Sea Divers, the first (and best) Mott The Hoople fan club.

A few years later, looking back on those early days, Ian Hunter wrote that "in 1969 Mott, among a few others, brought Friars to its feet in Aylesbury, and a cult built up around Dave Stopps, Pete Frame and the light show. And they were the days. Bowie thinks he started Friars, but Friars was years before his time." Indeed, it was the stir they caused on their Friars debut that prompted local writer Pete Frame, now universally famous for his *Rock Family Trees*, to give the band a big time write up in *ZigZag* #8, in an article entitled 'How The Hell Do We Get Started?'. In December, 1969, it was a question the band were often asking themselves.

1970 commenced with three month's worth of solid gigging, travelling up and down the M1 to clubs and college halls, playing a set comprising of songs from their debut album, plus versions of The Youngbloods' *Darkness Darkness*, and the Little Richard stomper,

*Keep A Knocking*. On the 21st of February, the BBC broadcast the band's debut session on the *Top Gear* radio show, with compere John Peel introducing the band, who then performed *Laugh At Me*, *At The Crossroads*, and a new number worked up in the studio the previous November, a Mick Ralphs rocker called *Thunderbuck Ram*. That month also saw the group make their debut TV appearance, performing *At The Crossroads* on BBC 2's *Disco 2* show.

**Above: Ian Hunter (photo by Barry Plummer)**

In March they travelled to Europe, making a brief appearance on the German TV show, *Beat Club*, before playing a couple of club gigs in Switzerland. In an interview with the *NME*, Buffin revealed that "on the Continent things are just beginning, and we're certain this is where the scene is going to emerge, especially in Germany." In the same interview Verden Allen commented that "when we go out on stage we just enjoy ourselves 'cos basically we are a rock band. And seemingly that is what they like."

April and May were taken up with further U.K. gigs, plus a second radio appearance, this time on John Peel's *Sunday Concert*, which was aired on the 3rd of May and featured Neil Young's *Ohio*, *Rock'n'Roll Queen*, plus a brace of previously unheard songs from the pen of Ian Hunter - *No Wheels To Ride*, *The Debt* and *Walking With A Mountain*, which were all recorded on the 23rd of April at the BBC's Paris Theatre.

At the end of May, the band flew across the Atlantic for their debut U.S. tour, which would keep them away from home for nine weeks. The album had been issued in the States at the beginning of the month by the mighty Atlantic Records, via a licensing deal with Island. In the early Sixties, Atlantic, by then universally renowned for its jazz, soul and R&B sides, had licensed its product via Decca, but the deal had proved to be strictly one way traffic. This subsequently meant they missed out on the British invasion of the early Sixties, and in particular Decca act, The Rolling Stones. In 1966, Chris Blackwell had offered the label The Spencer Davies Group, but Atlantic dropped them after their debut single *Keep On Running* failed to do the business chart-wise. The band subsequently switched to United Artists and enjoyed considerable success. Atlantic also had the option on The Troggs, but lost out to rivals Fontana around the time of the band's biggest Stateside hit, *Wild Thing*.

Finally wising up to what was happening over in Britain, the label signed up with entrepreneur Robert Stigwood and Polydor, giving Atlantic access to The Bee Gees and Cream. Signing Led Zeppelin before the band had even played live in the U.K., label boss Ahmet Ertegun began to chase English acts in a big way, snapping up Yes and Dada (featuring a young Elkie Brooks) in a deal with Island, which also gave them the catalogues of King Crimson, Emerson, Lake and Palmer, and Mott The Hoople. By the time Mott's debut was released, Atlantic had relinquished its independent status (it was swallowed up by the giant Kinney Corporation, whose other interests included parking lots and funeral parlours), but had increased its hipness quota among U.K. rock audiences by inking a deal to distribute The Rolling Stones new label.

Totally unknown Stateside, Mott The Hoople were relegated to bottom of the bill status on a series of concerts supporting the likes of Ten Years After, Jethro Tull, Quicksilver Messenger Service, and Traffic, although they had the bonus of being accompanied by Guy Stevens who, prior to a show on the 6th of June at Philadelphia's Electric Factory with The Kinks, took it upon himself to accompany Ian Hunter to a promotional interview at a nearby radio station. The singer remembered that "we were on a radio talk show with The Kinks. We were so nervous we hardly said a thing, but Guy just destroyed The Kinks, destroyed them to their face. They'd basically been saying that they'd rather be at home playing football and Guy just went mad, calling them hypocrites, saying they shouldn't be playing rock'n'roll if they felt like that, and they should just fuck off and play football and leave the music to the people who loved it. He had that total commitment to what he was doing and he insisted that you were the same."

Another notable gig on what was otherwise a pretty low key tour was on the 30th of June at an outdoor show in Crossley Field, Cincinnati, featuring Ten Years After, Mountain, Traffic, Grand Funk Railroad, Alice Cooper, Mott, and The Stooges. The show became famous in American festival folklore as the day head Stooge, Iggy Pop, somewhat the worse for wear chemically, jumped off stage and walked into the audience across their outstretched palms. The festival was filmed by NBC and broadcast on the 8th of August under the title, *Midsummer Rock*. The gig was also significant as the show where the band met two of what were to become their most devoted fans, Dee Dee and Daria. After seeing the band, they formed Hott Motts, a group of teenage girls who regularly followed the band from show to show, announcing their presence by hurling plastic breasts on to the stage.

Two days later in Boston, the group got involved in recording a public service announcement for the American Heart Association, who were urging people to avoid coronaries by having regular check ups. While Mott probably couldn't have cared less about some overweight middle aged American couch potato choking on his triple White Castle jumbo burger, it did give them the chance to slip a snippet of *Half Moon Bay* into an ad that was aired on 4,000 radio stations across the country.

In September, Island released the band's second album, *Mad Shadows* (a title Stevens had originally offered Steve Winwood), the recording of which had been done at Olympic Studios in Barnes during January and February. Originally titled *Sticky Fingers*, but changed at the last minute when Stevens got wind of a certain Dartford combo's plans to release a platter bearing the same name, it was hailed by Hunter as being "quite different from the first and is more or less representative of where we are now and what we play on gigs. Also, it is made up entirely of original songs," although a couple of years later, with the benefit of hindsight, he revealed that "I hate that album. I think I single handedly ruined the *Mad Shadows* record. I mean, you can hear the poor guys trying to play and I'm all over it; the singing is real bad. *Mad Shadows* was me egoing out. It is just stupid to me."

It seemed that the U.S. tour, while doing little to aid the band's record sales, had given their singer a taste for the big time, catapulting him headfirst into the rock star as spokesman for a generation ideal, a position he was at the time insufficiently qualified to apply for (hanging out with the new king of the Woodstock generation, Alvin Lee, whose band Ten Years After toured the States 28 times in only a few years and in the process virtually bankrolled the then tiny Chrysalis Records, hadn't helped). Singing like Dylan didn't make you like Dylan, although for a brief period, Hunter, who had now dumped the domesticated drudgery of a wife and kids for the seemingly hedonistic delights of a group crash pad off the Kings Road, seemed to believe so, although he did later own up to being "out of control at the time". Booze and pills were the guilty suspects, with Hunter maintaining that "the second album was much more difficult because Guy was giving us speed to stay awake. Instead of recording, we'd have 12 hours in the studio control room talking. We were a bit unhappy with some of the record because Guy went purely by feel."

Verden Allen recalled a total lack of preparation. "Mott went into the studio and sometimes we had no songs. It was just off the cuff." Terry Griffin was of the opinion that two months of trying to record an album during the day after driving all night long from a gig somewhere up North, grabbing a couple of hours sleep, driving off to do another show and then returning for more taping, put the band under undue pressure. "We were bitterly disappointed with *Mad Shadows*. It was followed by an unbelievably heavy tour schedule which left me exhausted and ill. I was sent home with glandular fever so bad that I couldn't touch things or sit up right. Island were still insisting that I go out on gigs."

As with the first album, the band had worked up a couple of medium paced rockers plus a handful of ballads, although record company pressure soon put paid to that. Hunter said at the time that "we would have liked to continue in the vein of the first album, but Island had seen what happened at live gigs when we did *Rock'n'Roll Queen*, and they felt we had to get more rock'n'roll."

The album opened with *Thunderbuck Ram*, a Mick Ralphs organ driven rocker taped on the 15th of November the previous year. The tune was originally over eight minutes long and had featured an extended organ solo in the middle, much to the disgust of Stevens, who edited it out without telling the band. *No Wheels To Ride*, a Hunter ballad reflecting the trials and tribulations of his recent marriage breakdown, had been recorded at Island's Basing Street studio, where Mott had been the first act to put the new 16-track desk through its paces. Waiting patiently outside the control booth while Mott did their stuff were Led Zeppelin, who, as soon as the studio was empty, went in and recorded their classic *Black Dog*.

Next up was *You Are One Of Us*, a jaunty kind of thank you to the fans who bought the first album (and hopefully this one) with a football terrace style singalong chorus ("You are one of us / Yes you are"), which led nicely into the side's closer, the Hunter penned Chuck Berryish rocker, *Walking With A Mountain*, a song its author recalled "was done out of panic; we needed a rock song . . . and that was written in the studio in about ten minutes."

Camped out next door at the time were The Rolling Stones, who had just commenced sessions for their *Sticky Fingers* album. Verden Allen remembered that "Mick Jagger sat down in our studio . . . and I remember he liked the high organ. He didn't actually sing on it, but he was in the studio when we did it." Hunter further elaborated, explaining "that's why it goes into The Stones thing at the end ("the Jumping Jack Flash / It's a gas" refrain) 'cos he was dancing in the control room." After seeing the self-styled "greatest rock'n'roll band in the world" at work, Hunter was amazed at the elephantine slowness of their creative process compared to the Guy Stevens' induced speedfreak race that his own band were being put through, saying that "The Stones got only one song in the six weeks we were there. But that was *Brown Sugar*." History actually has it that the Stones recorded *Brown Sugar* in December, '69, at Muscle Shoals, and by April '71 it was high in the singles chart, but you get the picture.

Side two of the album was particularly undistinguished, with Hunter's gospel tinged ballad, *I Can Feel* (notable for Allen's recorder style keyboard and Buffin's squeaky bass pedal), and Ralphs' stop-start country rock ode to better days, *Threads Of Iron* ("You are what you are / Yes you are / Yes you are"), featuring Hunter's anguished scream on the

**MAD SHADOWS/MOTT THE HOOPLE**
2nd album recorded live in the studio/produced by Guy Stevens
ILPS 9119

fade, a vocal pyrotechnic that would crop up with alarming regularity over the next few years eating up the majority of groove space, being blown away by the final cut.

The tune in question is credited to Hunter who, apart from Allen, was the only member of the band in the studio at the time. The singer has always maintained that their producer pulled a couple of invisible strings to extract what turned out to be a totally mind blowing performance. "Guy insisted that I just make up the song there and then, and out came *When My Mind's Gone*, a complete stream of consciousness." (Coincidentally, The Clash's Joe Strummer would claim that Stevens employed exactly the same technique on *The Right Profile*, a song from the band's classic *London Calling* album, Guy Stevens' last production job). Hunter expanded on his theory by adding that "when I'd finished, there was silence for a couple of minutes, and then Guy pulled the switch down and started screaming at the top of his voice. You wanted to work for him, to be great for him, because he was so excited when you were, and if you weren't he'd look at you with such a hurt expression."

Verden Allen, although suitably impressed by Hunter's off the cuff vocal dexterity, was a little sceptical of the singer's divine intervention theory, preferring to believe that "it was possible he was at home before and maybe had bits of it in his head. Then we were in the studio at the last minute and just did it."

Either way up, it was a monumental performance which distinguished what was otherwise a patchy album that, apart from its surreal brain scan style cover photograph (a painting of Frankenstein's monster driving a souped up Model-T Ford having been rejected) and the Baudelaire poetry on the back sleeve, was notable only for its virtual domination in the songwriting stakes by Hunter.

With cover designers Pete Sanders and Ginny Smith ensuring that he was the only member of the band pictured on the sleeve, the rest of the group began to feel that maybe Stevens was taking his vision of an "image minded and hungry singer" just a little too far. Verden Allen was unhappy with this and what he saw as an inferior product, but on confronting the producer he was fired. It was only a considerable amount of grovelling and muted apologies on his part, plus a tip of the collective cap from the rest of the band, that got him his job back. Drummer Griffin believed that "Guy felt, like love and hate, creation and destruction were inevitable companions" and that their producer was essentially "an explosion of energy, enthusiasm, ideas and inspiration," but that he also had a darker side to his character. "Equally he could be a crumpled heap of despair, tormented by his own shortcomings, seeking to destroy everything he loved and nurtured, himself included."

For the record, the group had a crack at taping Neil Young's *Ohio*, a song written by the godfather of grunge as a direct reaction to newspaper pictures of anti-Vietnam War protesters being manhandled by National Guardsmen at Kent State University on the 4th of May, 1970. Although the finished product was not deemed good enough for release, it remained a feature of the band's live shows for some time. They also had a go at recording a Hunter number called *Can You Sing The Same Song I Sing*, which dated back to his jobbing songsmith days, plus a group effort called *The Hunchbacked Fish*, which contained a heavy Dylanish lyric and a chorus revolving around the unlikely refrain of "The Hunchback Fish is weak / His money does not speak."

*"When Guy mixed Mad Shadows, I think that's when he was on some sort of speed. But I was very upset. I actually failed to smash the album, but I bent it back and forth. Guy was there with his mouth open in disbelief. I couldn't tell him in words. I tried to tell them, but nobody would listen."*

*VERDEN ALLEN.*

*"My position when we started selling out on gigs around the country with Mott The Hoople was that I used to get 15 quid a week. I had to pay eight quid a week maintenance to my ex-wife and two kids, so that left me £7. I used to have to give Mott four quid for one room in the house that we used to have down the North End Road. So that left me with three quid a week to spend. And I was supposed to be a fuckin' star."*

*IAN HUNTER.*

# CHAPTER 7

By mid 1970 the band had began to establish themselves as proven crowd pullers (Verden Allen believed that audiences first started to go wild after a gig at London's Roundhouse on the 21st of December, 1969, saying that "that's where we cracked it. It happened before, but that's when it REALLY happened"), but this audience reaction was not reflected in album sales. In Britain their debut reached number 66, while *Mad Shadows* fared little better, peaking at number 48. In the States, despite an enthusiastic write up in *Fusion* magazine by the legendary Lester Bangs, things were even worse, with the *Mott The Hoople* album dying a death at number 185, while its follow up, not released by Atlantic until November, was totally obliterated in the avalanche of festive albums and greatest hits packages that hit the racks at the end of every year.

The group made their second appearance on *Disco 2* on the 30th of September, performing *Rock'n'Roll Queen* and *Walking With A Mountain*, and on the 15th of October, they recorded a set for John Peel's *Sunday Concert* which was broadcast ten days later. Apart from these brief respites from the road, it was virtually half a dozen months of one night stands the length and breadth of the country, playing a set comprising of *Ohio, No Wheels To Ride, Walking With A Mountain*, Mountain's *Long Red, Thunderbuck Ram*, a new Hunter tune called *The Debt, Rock'n'Roll Queen* and, as an encore, a storming version of Little Richard's *Keep A Knocking*, although by April they had also found room to attempt a version of Jesse Colin Young's *Darkness Darkness* and Ian Hunter's *Original Mixed Up Kid*. The latter first aired on a short tour of Sweden in February which, apart from having to play in village halls to non-English speaking audiences, was notable on two counts; the first being that their Stockholm show on the 16th was broadcast by the local radio station (it later showed up as a high quality bootleg called *Long Red*), and secondly, after a particularly poor show at Uppsala University, the band had proceeded to jam for nine hours with folkies, Fairport Convention, in the words of Ian Hunter, "just to get our own back on the audience". Buffin remembered the tour as something of a nightmare, playing in tiny halls populated by local jobsworths and "as well as the staid and apprehensive audience, we had the problem of 'not being too loud please'."

On the 19th of March, 1971, Island released the band's third offering, *Wildlife*, which was unusual in the sense that the album was so laid back that even the band took the mickey out of it, preferring to nickname it *Mildlife*. Verden Allen believed that the problems the group had in putting the album together stemmed from his bust up with Guy Stevens over the *Mad Shadows* mix, and their subsequent decision to go it alone production wise. An increasing workload had led Stevens to let go of the managerial reins somewhat, with the slack being taken up by a couple of young hustlers, David Enthoven and Mark Fenwick, who had links with Island through their connection with King Crimson. "We went in to do *Wildlife* without Guy and that's when we were all sympathetic, and that's why it's very laid back," remembered Allen. Ian Hunter believed that "after the debacle of *Mad Shadows*, I think it was Ralphs, the voice of reason, who suggested we do some 'nice songs'. Mick was pissed off because I played such a big part in *Mad Shadows*. So Mick said 'let's produce the next one ourselves'."

With Stevens out of the frame, the door was now open for Ralphs to inject a mellower feel to the proceedings, with his contributions reflecting the influence of his current obsession, Buffalo Springfield, and it is this pre-Eagles mellow country rock sound which slugs it out over two sides for supremacy against Hunter's Dylan drenched angst ridden ballads. "After *Mad Shadows*, we wanted to be done with Guy," said Buffin. "There was no conscious veto of Ian's songs - he'd just not written much - and no rock stuff. Also, especially with Mick, there was a music snob thing that made us want to be 'serious musicians'."

The ever honest Hunter, always more than willing to push the latest product no matter how insipid, told the press that "I was actually embarrassed by *Mad Shadows*. It was badly produced and badly mixed, and I couldn't listen to it. I haven't even got it at home. It was a diary of bad periods we were going through at the time and was recorded live in the studio. The new album is lengths ahead musically. We put a lot more thought into it and a lot more time. The mix is so much better."

The lion's share of the recording had been done during the winter of 1970 at Island Studios, with the band (assisted by engineer Brian Humphries) producing themselves, much to the relief of Mick Ralphs. "It was the first time that the band got a say in what went on," remembered the guitarist. "On the previous two, we were just told what to do."

Opening with Ralphs' straight ahead rocker, *Whisky Women* (with its "Whisky Women / American lay" refrain it was a younger cousin to *Rock'n'Roll Queen* in the odes to Stateside groupies stakes), the album quickly slid into introspection, with Hunter's melancholy *Angel Of 8th Avenue* an instant reply to what had just passed. A plaintive lament to the ladies of the night, it had been written the previous June prior to a gig at New York's Fillmore East, while its composer "looked at Manhattan after a very drunken night at Nobodies in The Village", and featured (at the insistence of Ralphs) James Archer's haunting violin. The song tells of the relationship between the rock star and the groupie, its transience and shallowness ("I have so much to say / But so little time to stay") and, in hindsight, stands as one of Hunter's finest compositions, proving that when he stopped trying to be Dylan he could really get himself together.

*Wrong Side Of The River*, written by Ralphs, was a kind of other man's grass is always greener tune which had been recorded over at Olympic in February, but rejected for the *Mad Shadows* album, where it would have been totally out of place amongst the mayhem. Hunter's *Waterlow*, a song ostensibly about a park in London but actually about the pain of splitting from his children, was considered by many, including the man himself, to be one of the finest tunes he'd ever written. The sublime mood it created was totally ruined however by what followed - Guy Stevens' revenge (it was his only production credit) in the form of an embarrassing cover of Melanie's tribute to festival culture, *Lay Down*. Written by Miss Safka after she had appeared at Woodstock during a downpour, the song under its full title of *Lay Down (Candles In The Rain)*, had been a Top Ten hit in the States in May 1970, which is where the band first heard it. They had originally taped it with the

37

idea of putting it out as a single, but the song had been scrapped at the last minute when, in the true "progressive" style of the day, the group decided they were an album band. The song would raise its ugly head again a few years later unfortunately, when Island stuck it out as a single in Holland backed by *Whisky Women*, in order to cash in on the success of *Dudes*. On the trivia front it is worth noting that the track featured ace guitarist Jess Roden on backing vocals, who was repaying Hunter and Ralphs the favour they had done his band Bronco by playing piano and organ respectively on *Amber Moon*, a track from Bronco's *Ace Of Sunlight* album.

The listener, if not already confused by the vast array of conflicting sounds already thrown at them, was in for more surprises upon flipping the album over. Kicking off with session man Jerry Hogan's pedal steel drenched, *It Must Be Love* (with composer Ralphs leaning just a little too heavily on The Fabs' *All You Need Is Love* intro), and featuring a "that one's for you Brian" dedication to the engineer on the fade, they were then taken on a guided tour by Hunter through the ins and outs of teenage anguish in *The Original Mixed Up Kid* (who in his troubled mind "Sleeps with the ladies all night / Home in the morning light / To nothing", and then "Climbs into an empty bed / Pillows around his head / To hide the tears he sheds / For no one", lines which prompted its author to gush proudly that "it was probably one of the best songs I ever wrote").

Then Mick Ralphs gets everyone back around the campfire with another plea for the return of the good ol' days, *Home Is Where I Want To Be*, which Hunter, rather diplomatically, described as "my favourite track on *Wildlife*. Mick writes some good songs." Unfortunately, not too many of them were on this album.

By now Mott had forged a reputation as a solid live attraction, with their shows, while not always sell outs, never failing to be anything less than wild and raucous affairs. It was with this in mind that the group had toyed with the idea of releasing a live set from tapes recorded at a gig at Croydon's Fairfield Hall on the 13th of September, 1970, where they were supporting label mates, Free. In the end an over enthusiastic audience got the better of the P.A. and the idea was scrapped, although one track, a blistering ten minute plus blitzkrieg through Little Richard's dancehall screamer, *Keep A Knocking*, was salvaged, and

Mott
The
Hoople

a new album

'Wildlife'

ILPS 9144

OUT NOW

eventually found its way on to *Wildlife*. A regular encore, the band had been playing the song virtually from day one, and their fans knew it by heart. Originally double the length (it was edited down by Guy Stevens), Ian Hunter described it as "20 minutes of total stupidity - I loved doing that song live", and it went a long way in illustrating to the uninitiated what a great band Mott could be when they really put their minds to it. Explaining as to why no further concert tracks were forthcoming, Hunter said that "whenever we'd play live, it seemed like half the audience would get on stage with us. It was hopeless trying to record - the kids would be pulling leads out and knocking over mikes. I remember Pete accidentally knocking out a kid's front teeth with the bass one night because it was so crowded. I also remember kids with their heads in the bass drum."

No wonder then that with all these distractions taking place around them, the band found it virtually impossible to get a decent live sound down on tape, which is a real shame as, with the possible exception of *Whisky Women*, *Keep A Knocking* was the only track on the album to fully justify the inclusion of the word "wild" in the record's title. It was also the last real opportunity for the fans to catch a great live act thrashing through a rock'n'roll classic as by Christmas the band had dropped it from their set.

Although receiving positive reviews , particularly from the *NME* who described it as "a true labour of love (containing) a wealth of fine material which stands out in relief at a time when writers of quality are in abundance", the album stiffed at home (where confused fans stayed away in droves), but faired better in the States (it reached number 44) where the laid back country rock / Dylan groove was more accessible to West Coast A.O.R. ears. With this in mind, Island booked the group for a second U.S. tour in May, although in true hard luck story fashion, just when things were beginning to look up, "musical differences" beyond their control would deal them a cruel blow.

*"The buzz was in the air. It was like the early West Coast scene, and the kids were eager, happy and alive with anticipation. Mott were underground then. Why, I'll never know. We weren't into drugs but somehow the freaks related to us. We were green as grass, not too good, but enthusiastic . . . it was fun, nothing to lose. The press didn't like us but what the fuck? We were having a ball. The American press did like us but that was a fluke. We just didn't know what we were and what we had."*

*IAN HUNTER.*

*"During the first years of Mott The Hoople we had £2 per week each to spend, and we didn't feel poor. Watts and I got that much per week with The Anchors in 1963 and beer as well".*

*BUFFIN.*

## CHAPTER 8

On the 8th of March, while desperately trying to drum up some interest in *Wildlife*, Mott The Hoople had taped *Whisky Women, Angel Of 8th Avenue, Keep A Knocking* and *The Original Mixed Up Kid* for the BBC's *Sounds Of The 70's* radio show, which was aired a week later on the evening of the 16th. On the 11th of April, they also appeared before the cameras on *Disco 2*, which was transmitted by BBC 2 on the 16th too.

Free were always something of a volatile combination, torn between their earthy purist blues roots and the need to produce more commercial mainstream rock songs, none more so than *All Right Now*, which the band hated but had nevertheless been a massive hit on both sides of the Atlantic. Already established headliners on their own turf, Island were keen to break the band in the States, and so booked them on a heavy Spring touring schedule, with May being earmarked for a series of high profile showcase gigs with Mott The Hoople in tow. It was Chris Blackwell's idea to hitch Mott a ride on Free's coat tails Stateside, but everything fell apart when, after a pretty torrid Pacific Coast tour, Free split. This left Mott, who were unable to sell out the gigs on the strength of their name alone, with a tour now consisting of a handful of Detroit dates with Sweatdog and The Edgar Winter Band, plus a couple of hastily arranged East Coast shows supporting ELP, Sha Na Na and Grand Funk Railroad.

In her autobiography, *Man Enough To Be A Woman*, Jayne County gives an interesting insight into how marginal Mott were in the States at the time. In the Autumn of 1971, the then Wayne County was working as a DJ at Max's Kansas City, a popular New York hangout with the Warhol and MainMan crowd, owned by Mickey Ruskin. "Mickey wanted to keep the club very underground, so I was playing The Velvet Underground, the first Mott The Hoople album and the first Alice Cooper album . . . "

With the band twiddling their thumbs in New York, Blackwell decided to whisk them into a studio with legendary tycoon of teen angst, producer George Morton, something of a premier league tormented genius best known for his connection with Leiber & Stoller's Red Bird label and Spectorish style soundscapes with the queens of bad girl kitsch, The Shangri-La's. By now, Morton, nicknamed Shadow by fellow Brill Building songsmith, Jeff Barry, "because I was never where I was supposed to be", had been off the charts for some considerable time (his last major Billboard action had been Vanilla Fudge's psychedelic soul anthem, *You Keep Me Hanging On* in 1968) and inbetween he had

**Opposite page: Overend Watts (photo by Barry Plummer)**

developed something of a big time drink problem. Consequently not too much was done at the session, with only one song actually making it past the mixing desk and out of the studio door - a Hunter / Ralphs Stones-like workout called *Midnight Lady*. Featuring former Scene Club stalwart, Steve Marriot, then residing in stadium supergroup Humble Pie, on backing vocals, the song (with its driving beat and infectious "na, na, na, na" chorus) was deemed sufficiently radio friendly by Island's A&R boys to be released as a single (on June the 11th) in the U.K.. Backed by Hunter's *Wildlife* reject, *The Debt*, it received a gushing review from the *NME*. "*Midnight Lady* could do for Mott what *All Right Now* did for Free. Rough and ready and full of guts, this record drives with all the ferocity of a Force-9 gale, complete with a half sung, half shouted lead vocal, and a chorus supplemented by strong guitar and organ breaks. Full support from their fans could be enough to push it up the singles chart." The reviewers enthusiasm obviously rubbed off on Ian Hunter who told the 'paper that "if our current single hits the chart then we will release another album. If it doesn't we will make another single. We would like single success - but", he added somewhat sarcastically, "like The Stones and The Who USED to make."

With Island peddling the platter for all it was worth, the signs looked encouraging. Buffin remembered that "the sales were so promising that the BBC gave us a slot on *Top Of The Pops*." The band dutifully mimed to the record, confident that this was the break they had been waiting for, but "the day after the show aired, the single stopped selling".

On the 6th of July, the group taped yet another *Top Gear* session (aired on the 24th), this time performing *Midnight Lady*, *Angel Of 8th Avenue*, and Bob Dylan's *Like A Rolling Stone*, before appearing on Radio 1's *Rosko Show* (17th), where they debuted a couple of new numbers, *Darkness Darkness* and *The Moon Upstairs*. Although both songs had yet to appear on vinyl, *Darkness Darkness* had been in their set on and off since May, 1970, while *The Moon Upstairs* would receive its first public airing in August at Clacton's Weely Festival, a two day event featuring a dozen bands including King Crimson, T. Rex and The Faces. The gig turned out to be a total disaster for the band who were forced to play in the early hours of the morning to a totally phased out audience. Years later Buffin cringed when he recalled that "we were scheduled to appear between nine and 10.30pm (on the 28th). Our contract stipulated that if we did not get on stage within two hours of this approximate time, the promoters were in breach of contract. At 12.30am (on the 29th) we were still waiting and could have gone back to London to prepare for the Lyceum gig (scheduled for the 29th). As usual, like prize mugs, we went on stage at dawn."

As with most festivals, tape recorders in the audience were much in evidence and Mott's performance that day eventually showed up on bootleg. When Ian Hunter greets the early morning not so beautiful people with a hearty, "How's it been, alright?", the reply was "Fucking cold". The subsequent performance was somewhat subdued, although countering accusations that the band's minds seemed to be elsewhere, Buffin replied; "Uninterested? Knackered is more to the point."

On the 8th of July, the group played a headline gig at London's premiere classical venue, The Royal Albert Hall, supported by prog-rockers, The Amazing Blondel, to crowd scenes straight out of *A Hard Day's Night*. The P.A. blew up and the audience trashed the hall, leaving the group with a substantial bill for damages and the Hall's management slapping a total ban preventing any further rock acts from treading its hallowed boards. Coincidentally, it was at this gig that the band decided to throw 200 frisbees out into the auditorium, a stunt they had picked up at American gigs. But instead of throwing the frisbees back at the stage, the crowd - not knowing what the hell these mini flying saucers were - stuffed them up their coats to take home as souvenirs.

Undeterred, Island's P.R. department decided to milk the ban for all it was worth, and it wasn't too long before other venues refused to stage concerts by the band, prompting the record company to inform the press that in future the group would play gigs outdoors on their own inflatable stage. It was crass publicity stunts like this that caused Hunter to gripe that "we felt like the jokes of the label", although, unbeknown to the band, their time was almost up. Hunter, despite all the knocks, refused to remain anything other than steadfastly philosophical. "Once we start going downhill we will split," he told the

*NME*.  "At the moment we're going up and up, but once things start going downhill Mott will finish.  If the album doesn't do as well as the one before then its all over.  We will definitely split unless we get better."  Within six months, his statement would be tested to the limit.

*"Guy had a Ku Klux Klan thing on and the clock sort of got pulled off the wall somehow and I remember it hanging. We were all pissed. Guy brought wine in. I remember a big pile of chairs got slung all over the place and some of them were sticking in the wall of Studio 1 downstairs. It was complete chaos."*

*VERDEN ALLEN.*

*"Guy Stevens came in and said 'Wreck the studio', so we did, and we got the album done in five days. We needed to freak out. Brain Capers is the sound of a band freaking out."*

*IAN HUNTER.*

## CHAPTER

# 9

After the disappointment of *Wildlife*, Mott decided to reinstate The Masked Marauder Brothers (as Stevens and engineer Andy Johns were now calling themselves) for one last shot at immortality, although not before the now totally motorheaded producer had demanded £1,000 in cash upfront. And so it was that in one speed driven alcohol fuelled week in April, the band cut their fourth album, the recording of which, remembered Verden Allen (now sporting the nickname Phally . . . something to do with always playing with his big organ!), "was a bit like the first album. No overdubbing and the vocals were one take all the way through. It was crazy." Ian Hunter saw it as nothing more than "five days of total chaos . . . you can actually hear the pistols loud and clear. Guy Stevens and Andy Johns were dressed as highwaymen for the first two days in the studio with masks and guns." Bassist Watts believed that, clowning aside, the actual recording "was all done in about three hours. We just went into the studio, Guy got us drunk out of our heads, we just put the tracks down, then we smashed up the studio," - much to Chris Blackwell's disgust.

Ian Hunter remembered "meeting with him, right after he'd been to Nashville to record Steve Winwood, when he said to us, 'These people do albums nine to five. Why can't you people do that, instead of screaming and setting the place on fire?' He had us in tears."

Amazingly, despite all the madness and mayhem, 14 songs were taped, and eight made the final cut. Leftover were *One Of The Boys*, an acoustic growing up pains rocker by Hunter and Ralphs, Mountain's vastly overblown *Long Red*, a song that always worked well live but failed to come alight in the confines of the studio, a Hunter blues ballad, *Ill Wind Blowing* (which would have struggled to have made it onto the first album), *It'll Be Me*, a 1962 hit for Cliff Richard, Mick Ralphs' sensitive *Till I'm Gone*, recorded twice - once with a Ralphs vocal and once as a duet with Hunter - and Danny Whitten's homage to the heroin scene that would kill him within a year, *Downtown*.

Danny Whitten was a long time sidekick of the Canadian singer and slacker icon, Neil Young, and regularly played guitar in his backing band, but he was kicked off the rehearsals for Young's winter tour in November, 1972, because of his increasing reliance on heroin. He was paid off in cash and put on a plane back to San Francisco. As soon as the wheels touched the ground he was up and scoring a dose so lethal that within 24 hours he was dead. A devastated Young, who wrote *The Needle And The Damage Done* as a direct result of the tragedy, said that the guitarist's death "had stood for a lot of what was going on. It was like the freedom of the Sixties and free love and everything . . . it was the price tag. This is your bill."

Verden Allen remembers that "Guy Stevens came in one day with the *Crazy Horse* album and said 'look, I think you ought to do this track as a single'. There's a good video of that filmed in the Basing Street Studios. But the single was mushy and Ian wouldn't sing it for a start. He refused to sing that. It wasn't his cup of tea. It didn't really suit him. So Mick sang it." Buffin revealed that Guy Stevens "did initiate the recording of *Downtown*, but stormed out because it wasn't going how he wanted. Rather ill advisedly, we finished it off. Chris Blackwell said it was 'a certain hit'."

The song, backed with *Home Is Where I Want To Be*, was released a couple of weeks before the album. Contrary to the considered opinion of their label's boss, the single did nothing, its dismal sales consigning it to the record books as the hardest to find of all Mott singles.

Originally to be called *AC/DC*, the album's title, according to Buffin, "was ditched because we were worried about the sexual connotations", although it turned out that Hunter was hot on the idea "because really we were just as schizoid as ever, half fast and half slow." It was Buffin who inadvertently stumbled across the platter's actual title because "Guy Stevens couldn't decide between *Bizarre Capers* and *Brain Damage* . . . so I suggested *Brain Capers*."

Released on the 16th of November, it had *Melody Maker*'s reviewer reaching for the superlatives. "As in the past, this album is divided into two distinct categories; straight out tearing rock'n'roll . . . and their preference for loping slowies . . . this is a good album and all I can say is that I trust it gets the exposure it duly warrants."

One person who seemed to agree wholeheartedly with the reviewer's sentiments was David Bowie, a singer / songwriter of some repute, former soulboy, Tony Newley impersonator, bandwagon climber (his 1969 smash, *Space Oddity*, had hit the top the week of the first moonwalk) and now aspiring rocker / performance artist (he was fronting a band called Hype at the time). Bowie was enjoying his first taste of commercial success for years as writer of former Herman's Hermit Peter Noone's *Oh You Pretty Things* 45, which had recently seen some small time chart action. Verden Allen put his finger on Bowie's fascination with *Brain Capers* when he said that "it had an edge on it and an air of madness that he liked, I think. That's what turned him onto the band. We were going down really good at the time."

So good in fact that the former Mr. Jones was sufficiently impressed to send the band a rough demo of a song he had recently written called *Suffragette City*, although the group, in the light of the *AC/DC* debate, rejected it on the grounds that the lyric was a little too homophobic for their taste, with bassist Watts admitting that "we didn't do anything about it at the time. We played it and thought 'Dunno really'. It was a good song, but we didn't know if it was right for us."

Listening to *Brain Capers* today, it is easy to see why Bowie was so knocked out by its sound. Kicking off with a rabbit punch to the kidneys in the shape of *Death May Be Your Santa Claus*, a title lifted from a low budget underground flick about Black Panthers, this Hunter / Allen barnstormer concerned a lady who was clearly messing with her man's mind, giving the shaded one the chance to throw in a handful of his patented 'change / rearrange' couplets backing into the truly inspired "I don't care what the people may say / I don't give a . . . anyway" chorus. With the rhythm section purring like a finely tuned motor and Allen's keyboards wailing like a tom cat, *Death May Be Your Santa Claus* was pure good time boogie. Taped in one take, it is simply electric, right down to the triumphant "Whhhoooo!" at the end. (Note for trivia buffs: In 1972, long forgotten college rockers Secondhand released an album on Mushroom Records called *Death May Be Your Santa Claus*. The title track had actually been used on the film, and according to band member Arthur Kitchener, was originally called *Negro Brain*).

*Your Own Backyard* was a Dion DiMucci song which dealt with the harsh realities of the former teenybop idol's slow and painful rehabilitation after years of drink and drug abuse. The band had first come across it in 1970 when, after being taken from the *Sit Down Old Friend* LP, it was a minor hit in 45 form. In true Stevens' fashion, the song starts slowly and then builds as Hunter lays the trials and tribulations of a life lived at the bottom

of the bottle with just a handful of pills for friends, telling the listener in no uncertain terms that "You know / We're all losers in the end". Right on.

The album's other cover was *Darkness Darkness*, Jesse Colin Young's ode to paranoia which first raised it psychotic little head on The Youngblood's 1969 LP, *Elephant Mountain*. A slow brooding rocker which takes us on a guided tour through the outer limits of a mind that has clearly "Found the edge of silence / I am in depths of fear". Featuring some heavy duty guitar breaks from Mick Ralphs, who also handled the vocals, it was a song the band had down to a T after playing it live on stage since the Summer of 1970. For long time Mott freaks it was well worth the wait.

*The Journey* was a Hunter epic and, notably, his last real stab at impersonating Bob Dylan. Over his trademarked ham fisted piano and a plaintive organ refrain, the singer bemoans the high price he's had to pay for all those nights spent on the road ("I guess I lost just a little bit on the journey / And my mind's been split by little things that didn't fit on the way"), before the old Stevens trick of the fading scream is dragged out for old times sake as a cue for the rest of the band to kick into overdrive and riff the song into the ground.

Flip the record over and come face to face with one of Hunter's best ever tunes, the medium paced bar room boogie shuffle of *Sweet Angeline* ("The queen of the New York scene"), featuring a kooky lyric and a trickbag full of tasty organ fills (Allen's playing on this album was his best ever). It became an instant favourite among the fans and an integral part of the band's set for years to come, although the jaunty feel good party time groove is instantly forgotten with the arrival of *Second Love*, which heralded Verden Allen's much threatened but long awaited solo writing credit. The composer had initially recorded the vocal himself, but after the band voted his singing a little weak, the job was given to Hunter. Often misinterpreted as a story of a man carrying on an affair behind his partner's back, Allen put the record straight some years later when he said "it was religion. Nothing to do with physical love. I was going out with this girl called Elaine. I thought the world of her. She was a Jewish girl and the second love was religion." Emotionally torn ("I'm crossed between your second love / Some other one your thinking of / What is there now that I can do / I'll always feel the same about you"), Hunter screams out a plea for understanding over Stone's sideman Jim Price's wailing trumpet.

Following it was *The Moon Upstairs*, a Hunter / Ralphs full tilt rocker that sums up the singer's confusion and bitterness ("I feel neglected / Feel rejected / Living in the wrong time") at what he saw as the critic's apathy towards the band ("For those of you who always laugh / Let this be your epitaph"), before spitting in their collective faces ("We ain't bleeding you / We're feeding you / But you're too fucking slow"). Over a driving beat and heavy Hammond riff you can almost taste the vitriol. This was a song from a band who would take no more.

As with their debut, *Brain Capers* closes with a Guy Stevens' "composition". *The Wheel Of The Quivering Meat Conception* is basically aural porridge featuring Hunter's imaginary credit list ("The Mott The Hoople Light Orchestra have been playing some goodies and some newies and some oldies . . . ") plus that trademark scream again while the band arc out over the *The Moon Upstairs* riff, before the whole lot runs out of control and crashes over the cliff at 100mph.

The band spent October and November promoting the album on a headline tour of provincial halls supported by former Free vocalist, Paul Rodger's new outfit, Peace. With the exception of *Conception* and *Second Love*, they featured all the tracks from *Brain Capers*, plus proven crowd pleasers *Walking With A Mountain*, *Whisky Women* and, for an encore, the trusty *Keep A Knocking*. Hunter later recalled that at the Newcastle City Hall show on Bonfire Night, Buffin was uncontrollably drunk, which was no help at a gig where "disaster upon disaster fell upon us. He was so pissed, the roadies were feeding him black coffee during the numbers and stamping their feet in time with the beat so he could try to keep up. Needless to say he didn't. To cap it all, the organ broke down and we beat a hasty retreat, leaving a confused audience not knowing what was going on. If I die and go downstairs I would imagine hell to be like that particular gig."

The disgraced sticksman defended himself by revealing that "the problem was that I'd taken a slimming pill and didn't realise that it would react badly with alcohol. So I had some drinks, though nothing excessive, and it was okay until the reaction with the pill zombied me. My limbs were still obeying my brain - but rather slowly. It was all rather surreal . . . I was thoroughly ashamed of my stupidity and apologised to fans in a letter to the Newcastle press."

To accompany the tour, Island produced a lavish programme with extensive notes by Guy Stevens, who provided a potted history of the band from his (albeit warped) perspective, and then closed by saying that "believe it or not, Mott The Hoople as a group never wanted to go anywhere in an ambitious sense, which goes some way to explaining the curious enigma of a group with a simply enormous personal following who never quite received the recognition in the press that they both need and deserve in order to grow within the often limiting framework of a five man partnership. That they will get this recognition, in my mind, is not in doubt . . . there does not seem to be any foreseeable limits to their progress." For once Guy Stevens was to be proven wrong.

*"We had loaded ourselves with lots of debts, and we just had the feeling that we were going downhill. Rather than completely go to pieces, we thought the best thing would be to split."*
                                                                    BUFFIN.

*"It was a dead end . . . just a matter of time before Island sent us on a tour of Pakistan or somewhere."*
                    IAN HUNTER..

**CHAPTER**

# 10

On New Year's Eve, 1971, Mott recorded a rousing set at London's Paris Theatre for the BBC radio show, *In Concert*, performing *The Moon Upstairs*, *Whisky Women*, *Your Own Backyard*, *Darkness Darkness*, *The Journey*, and *Death May Be Your Santa Claus*. They then embarked on a further eight week slog around Britain's clubs and universities with only a week off inbetween (January the 24th to the 29th) which they used to good advantage, cutting demos on three new songs - *Black Scorpio*, *Ride On The Sun*, and *Moving On*.

In March they undertook a short European tour, only to find to their horror that Island's agency had booked them into a succession of crummy venues miles from major cities. It was at one such gig, in the shadow of the Swiss Alps, that the band decided to call it quits. Buffin recalled that "the group had continued just gigging around in circles until on the 26th of March, 1972, we found ourselves in a village outside of Zürich, playing in a disused gas holder that had cunningly been converted into a youth club. The Anchors would have thought twice about working that venue - let alone having to drive across Europe to do it." Ian Hunter also grimaced at the memory of "playing in Zürich in a gas tank that had been converted into a club, and we thought; 'If this is fame, forget it'. Our self worth was at an extremely low ebb. We genuinely felt that nobody wanted us."

It was a combination of a restless and apathetic crowd, equipment problems, and a couple of missed cues which resulted in a slanging match, culminating in Hunter throwing down his guitar and storming off stage. Upon their return home, the band were dismayed to find that they were contractually obliged to complete an April tour with young rockers Hackensack and comedian Max Wall, somewhat overenthusiastically billed as "The Rock'n'Roll Circus". Detecting signs of indifference on the band's part, Chris Blackwell informed them in no uncertain terms that "I've spent £2,000 on organising this for you. It's up to you. You don't have to do it, but I shall tell you now . . . if you don't do this tour I shall personally see to it that not one of you will ever do anything again ever in the music business."

An interesting footnote from the tour comes from a gig at London's Lyceum on the 19th of April. Hunter performed a ropey version of Dylan's *Mr. Tambourine Man*, but with new lyrics and a new title - *Hey Mr. Bugle Player*. It appeared to be a dig at the press and record companies who had ignored them in the past, but the song was so dire, it thankfully didn't crop up on Mott's set list again.

It was Overend Watts, believing that within a month he'd be joining the dole queue, but still in possession of the *Suffragette City* tape, who inadvertently set the wheels in motion that would dramatically alter the band's fortunes. "We got home from Switzerland and I thought; 'Well it's over, now what do I do?'. I rang David Bowie because he'd left his number on the tape. I wanted to know if he had any jobs going anywhere, we got talking for an hour, an hour and a half, and I was telling him about the group. He said; 'Look, I've got a song I've half written, let me ring you back in an hour or two. I have to speak to my manager'. He rang back and asked if I'd like to go and listen to the song. I said I didn't know how the rest of the group would feel, but I'd come over.  In fact he came and picked me up in a beaten up old Jag.  He was nervous to meet me and I was nervous to meet him. We went 'round to his manager's place in Chelsea, and he played part of *All The Young Dudes* on acoustic guitar".  The dumbstruck bassist couldn't believe his ears.  "You could tell it was a great song".

Scarcely able to keep the lid on his excitement, Watts hit the ground running.  "I came home and phoned the rest of the lads, and asked them if they wanted to hear the song.  We still had some gigs to fulfil, so we hadn't actually broken up, and when they heard the song they thought it was amazing."

It came as no surprise to Buffin to learn that his partner in rhythm had made the connection with the soon to be Ziggy Stardust.  "Watts was a Bowie fan from the early days.  Bowie, at the time when he had yet to make it, read in an *NME* interview that Mott were looking for songs.  He sent, during the *Brain Capers* sessions, a tape of *Suffragette City*.  We liked it, but did not feel it was a 'hit' or a 'Hoople-type' song.  Watts wrote to him and said 'Thanks'."

Watts invited Bowie to the bands 9th of April gig at Guilford Civic Hall, where Hunter remembers that "David was trembling.  He had this big thing, he thought we were very heavy dudes.  He used to tell people I was the head of a motorcycle gang and he had this very heavy deal about us." Nervousness notwithstanding, Bowie was instantly taken by the band's no holds barred show, which led Hunter to believe that "David was in love with us and wanted Tony (de Fries) to manage us.  David said to me; 'Trust him with your life'."

Trust him they did and, on the strength of a handshake, were taken under his wing. Amazingly, within days they were free from their recording contract.  Ian Hunter revealed that "we got off Island for virtually nothing, 20,000 bucks.  By this time, Island figured 'They're never gonna do anything'.  But we already had *Dudes* in the can.  We'd been down to Olympic in the middle of the night with David and done it.  And Blackwell didn't know" (Blackwell had the last laugh though as he still controlled the band's publishing through his Blue Mountain and Island Music groups.  It would be 1974 before CBS's April Music got a piece of the action.  Stateside, it was a similar situation, with Irving and Ackee Music cutting up the pie).  Tapes now clutched firmly in hand, Tony de Fries went in search of a deal.

*"He'd sit and talk for hours. A very fascinating guy, Tony. But when it came down to money it was weird."*

*IAN HUNTER.*

*"It would have been harder to imagine a more butch band than Mott were."*

*KRIS NEEDS.*

CHAPTER

# 11

When Mott The Hoople first stepped into his life, Tony de Fries was already on his way to building a business and managerial empire based, admittedly, on the talent (and earnings) of David Bowie, but structured primarily on his own financial wizardry and sheer unswerving belief in his own abilities.

Born in Rickmansworth on the 2nd of September, 1943 (his ancestors came from Friesland, hence the family name), Anthony de Fries was a sickly child destined to be cursed with all manner of illnesses during his early years. This left him bedridden for prolonged periods, eventually forcing his parents to enrol him in a special school for children with a delicate disposition. Upon completing his formal education, he joined the firm of Martin Boston as a trainee solicitor, and although he later liked to give the air of vast legal experience (Hunter once described him as "a lawyer's lawyer"), he was never actually called to the bar, and rose no further than the grade of litigation clerk. But what young Tony lacked in knowledge he made up for in front, especially after meeting pop svengali Mickie Most in 1964, when he helped the producer out in a dispute with one of his groups, Tyneside R&B belters, The Animals. It was around this time that he also came into contact with the legendary Allen Klien, then at Cameo-Parkway, but soon to gain universal fame (and notoriety) as both business manager to The Beatles and The Stones. It was Klien who took the young clerk aside and gave him a piece of music business advice that would serve him well in later years. "Son," he said, "Always keep your hands on the masters."

In 1969, de Fries joined The Association Of Fashion And Advertising Photographers (AFAP), becoming in time a vociferous and militant committee member destined to have many a run in with the giant IPC publishing conglomerate over photographers' syndication fees - so much so that at one point he even tried to form The Association Of Fashion Models, a union of beauties destined to be a non-starter in a profession not noted for its long hours and low pay.

It was through his dabblings with the fashion world that he first met impresario, Laurence Myers. A graduate of the old showbiz school of Parnes, Grade And Delfont, Myers was impressed by the young legal eagle's brash upfront style, and agreed to give him a start in the potentially lucrative pop music world. And so it was that in 1970, Tony de Fries became a partner in the GEM-Toby Organisation, renting out a couple of offices in Regent Street and going out hustling for potential stars. Myers quickly signed up Coca-Cola chart toppers, The New Seekers, and Gary Glitter, a.k.a. former Sixties also ran, Paul Gadd, who had spent many a night treading Hamburg's hallowed boards as Paul Raven & Boston International. They were a jack of all trades backing band who had once auditioned (and rejected) the young Ian Patterson, and who were now in the early throes of a last ditch attempt as the cartoon Glitter, hitching a ride on the coat tails of Glam Rock, a new teenybop craze instigated by another Sixties hasbeen, Marc Bolan.

For his side of the bargain, de Fries brought along David Bowie, an artist who had tried on more than one musical overcoat in his time but who the young hustler still had high hopes for. "He absolutely believed that David was, and would be, the greatest star in the world, and he acted accordingly," recalled Myers. In his autobiography, *The Leader*, Gary

Glitter remembered the GEM outfit fondly as basically "an umbrella type operation founded by Laurence Myers, a music business accountant who had seen that a great many producers, writers and artists' managers were in desperate need of hard nosed advice when it came to striking business deals with record companies. He set up the company in a block of offices and encouraged creative people to become part of it so that his specialised staff could manage their business for them - in return for a percentage - and leave them free to concentrate on the artistic side . . . it was the nearest thing the U.K. ever had to a Brill Building."

In August, 1971, de Fries had scored Bowie a deal with RCA at $37,500 per album on the strength that, according to his manager, he was going to be as big as Presley. At the time RCA were haemorrhaging dollars after investing heavily in black and white videos, only to find that their rivals over in the land of the rising sun had cracked colour technology, and consequently the Record & Tapes division had been told to get out there and shift some units. In their desperation to discover the next big thing, they swallowed de Fries' spiel hook, line and sinker - especially after he had extracted his boy from a two flops dead end contract with Mercury, by simply informing label boss Robin McBride that "if you require David to deliver the third album under his contract, we will deliver the biggest piece of crap you have ever had." McBride let Bowie go and gave de Fries the rights to his two Mercury albums (David Bowie and *The Man Who Sold The World*) for $20,000. Myers then went over to RCA and flogged the albums (but not the masters) for $37,500 each. Within 12 months both records were in the U.K. Top 30.

Bowie's first official release under his GEM contract was the critically acclaimed *Hunky Dory*, but it was the follow up, *The Rise And Fall Of Ziggy Stardust & The Spiders From Mars* that, along with a dramatic change of image, finally burst Bowie wide open. In February, '72, Bowie and his band, The Spiders, had premiered the album at The Toby Jug pub in Tolworth, Surrey, and on the 15th of July, a plane load of American journalists were flown over to Aylesbury Friars to witness the Ziggy show prior to a lavish reception at The Dorchester.

It was after this gig that Bowie commenced work at Trident Studios on what would become the *All The Young Dudes* album. By now Tony de Fries had sold Mott The Hoople to Dan Loggins at CBS for $50,000 (they had passed over on Bowie 18 months earlier and didn't want to get left out in the cold again, although Dale Griffin insisted that "RCA Records said that *Dudes* wouldn't hit - took too long to get to the chorus. But CBS went ape"), and with the money safely deposited in the bank (albeit GEM's), the group felt confident enough to have a crack at recording.

Mick Ralphs, victim of many a production deficiency in the past, reckoned that "it was a revelation working with him. He's a much more together bloke than people believe he is. He has a very firm sense of direction, total control over his own career, and he knows exactly where he's going. And yet at the same time he's always looking for new ideas - not just big ideas but little improvements, little ways of doing things better.

"He works very closely with Mick Ronson, and they are both very imaginative. Before recording us they both came to see us on tour, and to see the way we performed on stage - because they were anxious not to project us different to the way we were.

"Then, when we were actually recording in the studio, David was always looking for ways of making the sound that much better, for bringing out greater clarity, or using a different sound effect - some of them very strange. When we were recording the album he brought a blacksmith's anvil down to the studio one day. He had decided that he wanted the sound you get when you strike an anvil with a hammer. But instead of using the studio equipment to get something close to it, he got the real thing.

"Another time Ian Hunter told Bowie that he thought we could get a better handclap sound by recording the handclaps in the loo. Bowie responded at once, and got the technicians to install wiring and microphones in the loo, running the leads down the stairs to the studio sockets. Then we all stood in the loo, cramped together, shoulder to shoulder,

**Opposite page: Overend Watts (photo by Barry Plummer)**

clapping our hands, and recorded it. That's typical of him - every new idea has to be explored."

Ian Hunter was in total agreement, admitting that "before we teamed up with Bowie we were all a bit thick. We didn't understand the techniques of the recording studio - and we never worked as hard in the studio as we did with David. He's an incredibly hard worker.

"We learned different engineering techniques that no one had shown us before. In the past, if something had gone wrong on a session we just had to cope. But this time we were working with someone who had this basic knowledge, and could tell engineers exactly what he wanted. We were lucky because we learned all this from Bowie, but he must have been just as thick as us at one stage in his career - he must have learned it all from Ken Scott and his earlier producers."

Although the band were more than grateful for Bowie's assistance, one member felt that perhaps all the mutual praise for the producer was a little over the top. Just as he had once been the lone voice of criticism against Guy Stevens, so it was that Verden Allen remained totally underawed by the band's new mentor. "Don't forget", he reminded anyone prepared to listen, "He hadn't made it when he gave us *Dudes*. So helping Mott helped him as well."

*"They've never written better stuff. They were so down when I met them . . . everything was going wrong. They were so down I thought I was going to have to contribute a lot of material. Now they're in a wave of optimism and they've written everything on the LP bar that one Lou Reed song and the Dudes single."*

*DAVID BOWIE.*

*"David was one of the few people who can walk in and there's magic in the room. He has a very inquisitive mind, he's fast, and you feel that the guy knows more than you do so you put yourself in his hands."*

*IAN HUNTER.*

## CHAPTER 12

In the summer of '71, Tony de Fries had purchased an off the shelf company called Minnie Bell whose memorandums and articles of association listed its remit as to "employ authors and composers and to purchase copyrights and other rights in musical and dramatic compositions of all kinds". Under the terms of his agreement with Myers, he could, upon leaving GEM, take Bowie with him, with a rider that if the singer made it big then Myers collected $500,000. And so it was that on the 30th of June, 1972, de Fries changed Minnie Bell's name to MainMan (New York junkie slang for a dealer) and signed Bowie to what the artist believed was a 50/50 partnership. In reality de Fries owned 99 shares in the new company, with accountant Peter Gurber holding the other one. With Bowie tied down for a ten year stretch, de Fries wasted no time in hiring a bunch of Warhol performance freaks (spotted by Bowie performing in a play called *Pork*), bestowing titles upon them way above their ability or experience. But to de Fries that was unimportant. To be someone, you simply had to act out the part.

And so Tony Zanetta (a.k.a. Zee), long way off Broadway actor, became President, while former *16 Magazine* messenger boy, Leee Black Childers copped the Vice President's chair. Tony de Fries, according to the company records, had no official position in the organisation, although he wasted no time in setting his new charges, plus their vast array of hanger-on buddies, to work spreading the word among the hip New York crowd about Bowie. Soon MainMan had offices in Manhattan and Los Angeles, plus a suite in London's fashionable Gunter Grove, a place Kris Needs remembered well because "there were always people running around there; Mott, The Stooges, The Spiders. There was so much creativity going on."

History has shown that Tony de Fries had about as much sincerity as a snake oil salesman, but one thing he possessed in abundance was confidence, which oozed out of him in bucketloads. Buffin for one was bowled over. "I liked Tony. He taught us a lot about the business side of music, and we learned a great deal because he's very piratical. He's a rogue, but a 20th Century rogue who does things his way, without ever being the bully type. He got us out of our contract with Island, introduced us to CBS, and at the same time taught us one very valuable lesson . . . he taught us to be BIG TIME, to think like pop stars, to think beyond ourselves, and to reach for the stars rather than just keep plodding on."

These sentiments were echoed by other members of the MainMan circus. Bowie's wife, Angie: "He was high powered. Tony was interested in $20,000,000, not $20,000.

Tony de Fries had a very active mind and a desire to really do it. In the end I found him exhausting . . . he never tired."

RCA label boss, Dennis Katz: "de Fries was terribly difficult to work with, but great for his artists. He was very attentive to detail. He wanted to be in on the selection of the paper the album was printed on. He pushes and pushes and pushes . . . "

Lead Spider Mick Ronson: "He had a really nice voice, one of those voices that are really soothing. He'd sit and talk and he'd got such a great voice to listen to and he seemed to know about everything . . . I could have listened to him all night."

MainMan minder, Stuey George: "He'd tell us to go into a bank and ask to borrow £1,000,000 without knowing when you will pay it back, and the bank will lend it to you for your sheer cheek."

Long-time partner and mother of his daughter Fleur, Melanie McDonald: "He was the most amazing person I ever came across. He knew what he was doing all the time. I've never known him be wrong. He is right and he just knows it. He knows something's going to happen and it happens. It's amazing."

What de Fries did know was that in a no holds barred campaign to break Bowie in America, dollars were evaporating from the MainMan coffers at an alarming rate, a tidal wave that could only be stemmed by some serious chart action. With this in mind, Bowie worked his ass off on outside projects, most notably on Lou Reed's *Transformer*, Iggy's *Raw Power*, and Mott's *Dudes*, although it was in no way all one way traffic. Loopy Lou's credibility rating had never been in doubt, but working with Mott also did a great deal to enhance Bowie's reputation, especially among some of the more discerning critics, who had dismissed him as simply a charlatan hitching a ride on Bolan's glam rock gravy train. Mick Ralphs believed that the whole deal was one big learning process, with the honours being split an even 50/50. "I think he realised that he never did basic rock'n'roll very well, and that was part of the attraction to him in working with us - because at the time we were one of the rock groups he admired. He told us that we had a certain empathy with our audience which he liked, and we really were the old village hall rock group writ large, and that people seemed to be afraid of us because our image was merciless. The other thing is that he liked us for preferring the sort of music we did, old style rock, to his music. I think he learned something from us, the raunchiness we had always had and which he lacked. It was a good experience working with him because I think we learned from each other."

For Ian Hunter, it was the sheer joy of working with a happening outfit that impressed him most of all. "The thing was that David as an artist was in charge of everything - he was in charge of his management, in charge of his agency and in charge of his recording company - and he was thus totally in control of his own destiny, which was something we had not seen in any other singer or musician before." (If this seems somewhat over the top, it can probably be put down to Hunter's sheer joy at finally getting a sniff at some chart action. As has previously been noted, Bowie was under the impression he was an equal partner in MainMan, but wasn't. His gigs were booked by the mighty William Morris agency and his records released by the giant RCA conglomerate, neither of which listed the former Mr. Jones as a major shareholder. As for his destiny - within 18 months he would be trying to extract himself from the clutches of Mr. de Fries).

"Now we have the same relationship with everyone who surrounds us," Hunter continued. "They all work FOR US. They ask us before doing anything in our name, and we have no quarrels with management or record company, because we all know what the relationship is. One big debt we owe to de Fries is introducing us to CBS, who have been marvellous to us.

"We've learned all this because this is how Bowie makes it work for him - even down to the little things like having to suss out the artwork for your next album sleeve before you even start recording the album, because it will take longer to arrange the printing of the sleeves than the actual production of the records themselves. Thus, if you want to have your say, all this has to be set in hand well in advance - otherwise it's all done as a rushed job by the record company."

This mutual admiration society was cemented by Bowie himself, who thought that "they were being led in so many different directions, because of the general apathy of their management and recording company. Everybody was so excited about them when they first came out, but because they didn't click immediately it fell away. When I first saw them I couldn't believe a band so full of integrity and a really naive exuberance could command such enormous followings and not be talked about," although Kris Needs for one believed that Bowie's real motive in becoming involved with Mott was nothing more than a healthy dose of old fashioned hero worship. "David looked up to Ian Hunter. In a way he saw himself up there, with the same control over an audience as Ian always had."

It was Hunter who was probably closest of all to the mark when he dropped his guard for a second to say that "the type of thing that Mott had that Bowie never had was humanity. I think he was upset because he never had riots. People were too polite to riot at his concerts."

The *Dudes* 45 was released on the 28th of July, 1972, and almost immediately began picking up heavy airplay, prompting the band to get out on the road for a handful of showcase gigs designed for the sole purpose of letting everyone know that they were back and that this time they meant business. With the MainMan press office switching into overdrive, it was no surprise to find Ian Hunter's mugshot plastered all over the music press, bold as brass and arrogant as hell, peppering interviews with quotes like, "It was obvious it was a hit" and "he offered us *Suffragette City*, and I said it wasn't good enough. I knew at that point that any single we put out would have to be a motherfucker."

A right motherfucker it turned out to be too, going top five by late August and giving the band a second bite at the *Top Of The Pops* cherry. Buffin sensed the band were onto a winner one day in the studio when "Mickie Most put his head around the door of Olympic Studio 2 and said, 'You've got a hit there'. 'Number one', said Bowie. 'Hhmmm . . . Number three', said Most. He was right".

Buffin was also quick to dispel any rumours to the tune that the band were merely Bowie's puppets, revealing that "his only real involvement was doing the incidental backing vocals on *Dudes*. To record it, he played it to us, we played it back to him. I believe that Ralphs wrote the guitar intro. Ian did the vocal. All the ad-lib bits were his own. 'Hey, you up there' was a steal from a regular comedy sketch on *The Billy Cotton Bandshow* where Billy Cotton was addressed by an alien in a spaceship; 'Hey, you down there with the glasses . . . '"

There's an old music biz saying that behind every hit there's a writ (as well as a cheap cash-in, this time in the form of Island's spoiler *Rock'n'Roll Queen* compilation, worth collecting only for the pop-art Philip Castle cover), and it was worries over possible legal action from Marks & Spencer that prompted a partial re-recording of the song. Bowie had originally written about 'Wendy stealing clothes from unmarked cars", but Hunter decided that "Marks & Sparks" sounded better, although as soon as the single began picking up airplay, CBS panicked at the thought of a possible lawsuit from everybody's favourite High Street store, and quickly despatched Hunter to Trident Studios with Bowie and his producer Ken Scott to re-record the offending verse for European and American release. They needn't have bothered as the men in suits at M & S didn't even bat an eyelid, and it is the original version that is still the most commonly heard.

The *Dudes* album, which followed hot on the heels of the single, came as something of a surprise to many long time fans (including Fusion's Lester Bangs, who thought it was a little lightweight), featuring as it did a new, tighter Mott, devoid of any rough edges, and sporting a drastically cleaned up sound. The record opened with The Velvet Underground's *Sweet Jane* (Bowie was a long time groupie of the band), although a somewhat dazed and confused Hunter later admitted that "I couldn't understand what the song was about, not being a New York fag."

Mott's high stepping uptown uptempo version was a million miles away from the composers original slower heroin hazed blueprint, although this was mostly down to Bowie. Buffin remembered that "he played it to us and we played it back - as with *Dudes*. We had

## on tour!

Dunstable Civic Hall September 15
Manchester Free Trade Hall September 16
Hanley Victoria Hall September 17
Middlesbrough Town Hall September 9
Sheffield Top Rank September 21
Dunstable Mayfair Entertainment Centre
September 22
Liverpool Stadium September 23
Carlisle Market Hall September 24
Wolverhampton Civic Hall September 25
Leeds Town Hall September 26
Birmingham Top Rank September 27
Coventry Locarno September 28
Bristol Top Rank September 29
Malvern Winter Gardens September 30
Chatham Central October 2
Brighton Top Rank October 4
Margate Dreamland Ballroom October 6
Southampton University October 7

## on record!

Mott The Hoople
All The Young Dudes
On CBS 65184
All The Young Dudes. The smash single that's now the title of an incredible Mott The Hoople L.P. Ten great tracks, including the Lou Reed classic 'Sweet Jane', from one of the tightest-workinest-bands-in-the-land. Produced by David Bowie.

Home. Their second album.
On CBS 64752
For the past year they've been bringing audiences to their feet at concerts up and down the country. (Not an easy thing to do when you're on the same bill with the likes of Argent, Rod Stewart and Led Zeplin.) Now Home have a new L.P. filled with tight, funky rock sounds for you to sample.

no idea that the original was so slow. Lou Reed went white when he heard how fast it was."

Next up was *Momma's Little Jewel*, a Hunter / Watts composition previously demoed as *Black Scorpio*, and now sporting a funky arrangement courtesy of Mr.B. With its catchy riff, infectious chorus and Bowie's asthmatic slow down to stop sax at the end, it was a cool put down on a spoilt little lady who was "Momma's little jewel / Just out of school / And fresh from the nuns who made you / Who believed she knew all the right moves". That is until she bumps into the streetwise swagger of Hunter, who informs her in no uncertain terms that "Momma's little jewel / You've got the rules / But I'll be the one to educate you". The song stutters straight into *Dudes*, sounding somewhat muffled against the more up-front mix of the rest of the album, probably because it was recorded months earlier in a different studio. As the teenage rampage fades out, with its fanfare, "All the young dudes / Carry the news / Boogaloo dudes / Carry the news" chorus - *Satisfaction* meets *Hey Jude* - in comes the groin kick of *Sucker*, a Ralphs / Watts tune with a snarling Hunter lyric, oozing out from under the floorboards. "Hi there / Your friendly neighbourhood sadist / Come to take you for a ride", sneers Hunter, before taking us on a guided tour through the back alley of depravity that constitutes his current relationship, the cabaret of which consists of 'Two tiny purple hands / Crawling out across the floor / All I could hear was a voice / Gimme more, more, more", leaving the listener in no doubt that Hunter's main squeeze had "No pride in her heart / I never fail / She's a sucker". Featuring some classy mandolin playing plus a searing solo from Ralphs, the song was a raunchy ride through the wild side, and destined to become a regular feature of the group's live shows for the next couple of years. Buffin for one though felt that the end product was not a patch on what it could have been. "*Sucker* sounded phenomenal when first played back at Trident," said the drummer. "The heaviest, hardest hitting track we'd ever done, and just how we wanted it. When mixed it was piss weak - led by Bowie's acoustic guitar and no bollocks."

Another number which came in for criticism from the sticksman was *Jerkin Crocus*, a song allegedly about an ex-girlfriend of Overend Watts, but more likely, according to Mr. Griffin, "named after Creepin' Jesus, a wild tramp who lived in the Ross area during the Sixties. His name was changed by Watts and Fishpool, in the same way that Sniffin Griff Griffin - that little bugger Sniffin - that little sniffer Buffin - Buffin. So Creepin' Jesus was turned into Jerkin Crocus."

The song, a Hunter penned Stones-like shuffle about a young lady who liked nothing better than "Just a lick on your ice cream cone" and whose ambition appeared to be nothing less than "A judo hold on a black man's balls" (very painful!). Buffin said that "at the end of *Jerkin Crocus*, Ian says, 'That's much better'. He was referring to the powerful, controlled feel of a track. That is not apparent in the mixed version. All the power and size have been removed."

That didn't stop Jeff Lynne from lifting the riff wholesale for ELO's *Ma Ma Belle* single though.

The controlled aggression of Side 1 spilled over the record and into *One Of The Boys*, the full length version of the *Dudes* B-side, a Hunter / Ralphs workout sporting a riff that the guitarist would shortly put to more profitable use elsewhere. The tune had originally been demoed on the 24th of January at Basing Street Studios with acoustic guitars, but after Bowie decided it sounded a bit on the limp side, Ralphs beefed it up on electric. Apart from that, the song sticks closely to its original arrangement, with the exception of a couple of sound tricks tacked on later. Once again it was Buffin who was less than complimentary about the producer's role, complaining that "Bowie did nothing to *One Of The Boys* - just hustled us through and added effects and the telephone thing . . . "

Verden Allen's *Soft Ground* followed, an organ led tour through the composer's psyche, and his fears that the MainMan connection would, in the long term, bring nothing but harm to the band, where there were "Too many people about / Telling me what to do with myself", resulting in the organist finding it "Hard to get around / Walking on soft ground". Allen truly believed that the Bowie foundation was shaky and did not shirk from making his feelings known, so much so that Leper Messiah began to whisper in Hunter's ear about a weak link in the chain.

Mick Ralphs' vocal spot, *Ready For Love* (and its acoustic guitar showcase segment *After Lights*) was another track destined to become a live favourite. Over a simple two chord riff, the guitarist sang his patented angst ridden lyric about "Walking down the rocky road / Wondering where my life is leading / Rolling on / To the bitter end" (also see *Home Is Where I Want To Be*, *Wrong Side Of The River*, etc,.), with Hunter wailing out the bridge, urging the damsel concerned to "Give it to me / You know what I'm talking of / Give it to me / I'm ready for love". This was stadium rock 15 years before Bon Jovi.

The album closed with Hunter getting all reflective at the ivories on *Sea Diver*, a song demoed earlier that year rather unsuccessfully as *Ride On The Sun*. The lyric dealt with the singer's struggle to achieve artistic credibility in the eyes of the rock critics, and was underpinned by a classy string arrangement courtesy of Mick Ronson, who hit it off instantly with Hunter but, according to Buffin, kept a cool distance from the rest of the band.

"He wasn't overtly friendly during the *Dudes* sessions," remembered the drummer, adding that "we took it that he was busy. Besides, we did hold him in some high esteem and accepted that he might not wish to trouble himself with us."

With the single riding high on the crest of a chart wave, and the album (featuring a Great Gatsby style cover courtesy of Bowie's old school pal, George Underwood) picking up favourable reviews and encouraging sales, Tony de Fries was more than anxious to get the band back out on the road. Apparently Bowie was keen to have them support him, but Hunter put the blocks on it, refusing to play second fiddle "with a lousy sound system" for 20 minutes. "You pass like a mild irritation in the night", he said. "I knew what the bugger was up to."

As far as Hunter was concerned, Mott were as big in Britain as Bowie (they certainly had a more fanatical following) and there was no way his hard earned and long awaited moment in the spotlight was going to be denied him. As he said on the fade out to *Dudes*, "I've been waiting for this for years . . . " So instead the band Home were roped in as support to Mott as they gigged town halls and Top Ranks throughout September and into October. They were accompanied on the tour bus by the legendary king of Hollywood sleaze, producer Kim Fowley, whose hanging out with Hunter had actually resulted in the penning of a few songs, one of which, a tune about Hollywood & Vine, was at one time considered as a possible candidate for the group's next album.

MainMan wanted the band over in the States as soon as possible in order to hitch them a ride on Bowie's second U.S. tour beginning in mid-October, but work permit problems, coupled with Hunter's increasing reluctance to stand in Bowie's shadow, meant that the tour, scheduled to kick off in Atlanta, was put on ice. Instead the tour was restructured for the following month to take in five weeks, with the band being booked in at the Hyatt (a.k.a. Riot) House (where, within minutes of checking in, Hunter noted that "some chick called Rachel is ringing Pete once an hour and Phal's having trouble getting rid of a bird he said hello to three years ago"), prior to opening at The Hollywood Palladium on the 18th of November. Then, in typical MainMan zigzag fashion (they were total novices when it came to planning U.S. campaigns, with many of their artists forced to travel thousands of miles across the continent, from east to west and back again, with long costly lay-offs inbetween), Mott shifted 3,000 miles north to Philadelphia and the east coast before heading back through Indiana, Texas and, finally, Tennessee.

Along the way there was constant speculation as to where the next single was coming from, with Hunter confident that "it seems likely we'll do it in New York in early December as David's tour will be over by then and we should be in the New York area."

The majority of the gigs were support slots (the band, despite this being their fourth tour, were still relatively unknown), although their gig at the Tower Theatre, Philadelphia, introduced by a breathless Bowie after a 200 mile cab ride, was broadcast by local radio, and went a long way to breaking the band in the eastern territory, where they had always had a small but solid fan base. The Philly gig was their first ever bill topper Stateside, and, due to the excellent acoustics of the auditorium (Bowie recorded his first live album there), the radio broadcast of the gig on the 4th of December was top quality, prompting the inevitable issue on bootleg as *Midnight Lady* (a.k.a. *Mott The Hoople With David Bowie*).

Kicking off with a storming version of *Jerkin Crocus*, the band then tore through *Sucker*, *Hymn For The Dudes* (a new song Hunter dedicated to the six victims of a shoot-out in the city earlier that day), *Ready For Love*, featuring a blinding Ralphs' solo, a poppy *Sweet Jane*, a rather shaky *Sea Diver*, before pulling it back with a barnstorming finish consisting of *One Of The Boys*, *Midnight Lady*, a Bowie led version of *Dudes*, and for finishers, a laid back stroll through *Honky Tonk Women*. The shows were now bookended by the L.A. Symphony Orchestra, conducted by Leopold Stokowski, and performing *Jupiter* from Holst's, *The Planets*. Hunter explained that "Pete recorded *Jupiter* on a cassette once. We played it over the P.A. at a rehearsal and it sounded so good we've used it as an introduction ever since."

Tony de Fries, meanwhile, was involved in some heavy duty hustling, including a "no interview" policy designed to build an aura of mystique around the band, a tactic that worked well with Bowie and his alien from another planet guise, but one which didn't sit too comfortably on the shoulders of a band who had always gone out of their way to build up a rapport with the press. There was also a noticeable shift in dress code, with denim waistcoats, granddad vests and flared denim jeans being ditched in favour of a more 'glam' orientated style (the most noticeable of which was Watts' thigh length boots and silver sprayed hair (according to Hunter "we've got to look groovy so our manager . . . gave us £100 each to buy clothes. That's okay, but the clothes are all shit - Carnaby Street, Ken Market, Kings Road - ridiculous prices for rubbish that doesn't last five minutes"), although Buffin still believed that their manager's strategy taught them some invaluable lessons. "Island's policy had always been to 'plod on and you will get to the end of the road'", he said, remembering the hard slogs of their early days. "But Tony's attitude to it all was very different. When we did our American tour he told us to behave like stars - even though we hadn't made it yet. He arranged the whole star thing for us - the best hotels with two limousines waiting at the door. It was an invaluable experience, but of course we paid for it. The cost was added to our bills. But it made our attitude very different. It made us feel that everything was possible."

With de Fries and / or his leg men Childers and Zanetta travelling with the band for most of the tour, things ran far more smoothly than on previous excursions where the band, not being represented by Island in the States, had little if any managerial muscle behind them, and were consequently roped into many a dodgy gig. This time around they were wrapped in the security blanket of Tony de Fries and his hard-nosed fantasies, which meant not having to think twice about pulling out of some of the smaller gigs, especially where they were lower than third on the bill (unlike the U.K., where the standard gig consists of headliner and support act, it is not uncommon in the States to have half a dozen or more bands sharing the same bill), a policy that left Hunter for one suitably impressed. "I simply think he's the best manager since Colonel Tom Parker. And I will continue to think that whether we continue our relationship or not. The fact that we're not signed to him in any way should indicate the trust involved."

This cosy arrangement wasn't for lack of trying on de Fries part, and fails to reveal Hunter's nagging distrust about the Bowie deal. The manager had given Hunter a set of contracts to distribute among the band in the hope that (Hunter's words) " . . . a couple of suckers would sign . . . I immediately collected them and took them home and put them under the piano stool. Now and again he'd say 'Where's the contracts?', and I'd say 'somebody forgot'". Although he did approve of the ego tripping and how "he's going to make us stars", a closer inspection in the mirror forced him to concede that the boss had "got a job. I mean, I want to be a star, but I keep thinking we're just ordinary blokes, we don't have the killer instinct. I can't keep myself continually composed like Bowie does. It's like trying to keep your stomach in. Mine flops out occasionally."

*"By now Bowie was becoming so huge that de Fries was having to give him all his time, and he couldn't really cope with us as well."*

*MICK RALPHS.*

*"I think the one thing that impressed itself upon us more than anything is that a group must be the master of its own destiny."*

*IAN HUNTER.*

CHAPTER

# 13

The band flew back to England after playing a triumphant end of tour gig at the Ellis Auditorium in downtown Memphis, which featured a second lead guitarist in the shape of future Eagle, Joe Walsh (complete with foot in plaster), whose band Barnstorm were that night's support act. The evening actually ended with a drunken Allen and Hunter blagging their way into the grounds of Graceland, an escapade fondly remembered by the organist, who recalled that "when I got home I'm in the pub the next night in Hereford and I said to this friend, 'Incredible last night. I nearly got shot at Elvis Presley's house', and they all thought I was round the bend."

Accommodation had stepped up a rung or two since the days of the communal crash pad, particularly after Mick Ralphs had fled the roost in favour of a Shepherds Bush lovenest with girlfriend Nina, who Hunter, ever the ladies' man, described as "delicate and sincere . . . her control over animals has to be seen to be believed". Allen and Griffin had also relocated to West Kensington bedsitters, while Watts and his lady Pam, both into antiques and chess in a big way, had a "one roomed junk shop" in Hampstead. As for Hunter, he had recently married an American / Austrian girl called Trudi (they met during Mott's 1970 U.S. tour), had a cat called Saucer, a dog named Solveig, and a black and gold Anglia with big tyres, all around at his tiny flat in Wembley.

The plan was to rest up over Christmas and then meet in the new year to begin recording demos. It was with this in mind that the Hunters travelled down to Northampton to spend the holidays with a few of Ian's friends. It therefore came as something as a surprise when the singer, suffering first degree jet lag as well as a major league hangover, received a phone call from Bowie begging him to come down to Haddon Hall (the thin white one's residence at the time) for some urgent discussions on the future of Mott. Thinking that Bowie had finally got around to the next single he had been promising to deliver for the band, Hunter dragged himself into his car and wearily headed on down to the old Edwardian house at 42, Southend Road, Beckenham. Hunter genuinely believed that the urgent topic of conversation would be *Drive In Saturday*, a tune Bowie had written with the band in mind, and had played to the singer a couple of weeks earlier (the 10th of December to be exact) at New York's Warwick Hotel. Hunter, with only a very rough demo to go on, was knocked out by what he reckoned was "a beautiful song which grows on you. It's Dylanish and it's got a hell of a chord rundown."

He was therefore extremely peeved upon his arrival at chez Bowie to find the carrot topped one and his clothes designer, Freddi Burretti (a.k.a. Arnold Corns), playing peek-a-boo from behind the sofa. Hot eyed and tour frazzled, Hunter realised that he was the victim of a power trip on the part of his producer. Feeling a first class prat, he stormed out. "Angie (Bowie) was embarrassed and upset . . . it was either smack him or ignore him. I didn't want to smack him because of Angie, so I just ignored it."

Hunter walked away feeling used, and, given time to reflect on the long drive back to Northampton, came to the conclusion that Bowie was nothing short of a rock'n'roll

Dracula who "sucks what he can and then moves on to another victim", although the official explanation on the cooling of relationships between Bowie and the band was put down to the fact that "when David got enormous in America and then Japan, he (de Fries) was gone and we had no effective management at all. We were ringing him from England . . . we were impatient and he couldn't handle two things at once so we were getting neglected. So we said, 'Well, let's call it a day' and he said, 'O.K. great'." Implausible as this might seem, bearing in mind many managers have had more than one big iron in the fire (Brian Epstein, Elliot Roberts, Robert Stigwood, and so the list goes on), in MainMan's case this seemed to be the norm. Over the next few years, the careers of The Stooges, Dana Gillespie, Annette Peacock, Wayne County, Mick Ronson, and a young John Mellencamp would all be sacrificed in the never ending quest for the next Bowie dollar.

Buffin remembered the weeks after the U.S. tour as being ones of indecision. "We were promised *Drive In Saturday* as a follow up to *Dudes* - but Bowie and Mott's careers were very parallel in America. In fact we were ahead in national terms - and I think he felt that de Fries couldn't serve his and our interests. So the MainMan involvement began to distance itself. Wages became erratic and contracts problematical. Suddenly it cut off and we were left to the mercy of CBS who suddenly got cold feet. So did Ian - he panicked and decided he'd 'gone solo', but we could play on his record. So we went to AIR Studios and did *Honaloochie Boogie* and *Ballad Of Mott* as Ian's backing band. The tracks came out beyond our wildest dreams and the solo career was forgotten . . . for the time being."

It seemed that Hunter had suffered an attack of nerves after the MainMan split and believed that the band, without decent management support, would end up back where they were in March, '72. The arrival of Bob Hirschmann, a talented young booking agent looking to get a toehold in the management game, coupled with the quality demos the band had knocked together from Hunter's hastily scribbled songs, convinced the shaded one to keep plugging on. He felt totally let down by MainMan and wasted no time in venting his feelings in the music weeklies, telling the *NME* that, "I can't tell you how badly we wanted people to know that David didn't create this band. He'd saved our asses, no two ways about it, but it was a jigsaw puzzle and he'd just put in some of the pieces. We were scared all the time after *Dudes*, wondering if we'd be able to come up with a single that would chart in England (in the States, Columbia had issued *Sweet Jane / Jerkin Crocus* as a single, but it failed to show on the chart, unlike *Dudes* which made it to number 37). If we did something without Bowie and it died the death . . . "

But it wasn't only the public that the band had to win over. Hunter was acutely aware that "we had to convince Clive Davis (Columbia's head honcho) that we knew what we was doing. He came over in a panic. He thought we were spending Columbia's money inadvisedly. Clive Davis came up with Fred Heller as manager for America. He also wanted us to use Bob Ezrin as producer as well, but we knew we'd finally found the clue to producing and arranging ourselves."

There was a sense in what Davis was saying. Fred Heller, who operated from sumptuous offices situated in Dobbs Ferry, off Manhattan island, was an old hand on the U.S. concert scene and had the necessary connections to ensure the band would receive maximum exposure on any future tours, while Ezrin was at the time red hot, having just come off a run of million sellers with Alice Cooper. After being turned down by Mott, he went off to work on possibly the most difficult album of all time, Lou Reed's monumentally bleak, *Berlin*. Hunter was also not being totally truthful when he said the band always wanted to produce themselves. They may have turned their noses up at the prospect of working with a Canadian, but they had no reservations about spending studio time with one of Britpop's prime movers, Roy Wood. They only opted to record themselves after the former Move and ELO frontman's involvement with his new band Wizzard meant that he was unable to commit himself to outside projects.

The band booked time at AIR Studios for January and February and commenced working up a batch of songs written primarily by Hunter, and heavily influenced by events on the Dudes tour. While the rest of the band grudgingly accepted Hunter's role as numero uno tunesmith within the fold, organist Verden Allen, who was by now finally finding his creative feet and writing in earnest, demanded room on the record for a couple of his tunes. When the band passed on his songs, he threw a tantrum, which was dutifully ignored. Finding himself backed into a cul de sac, he decided to quit. "I left because I honestly don't think anybody knew what to do at that particular time," he recalled some years later. "Because Bowie wasn't coming back . . . I said, 'I'm leaving the band. I'm off'. I'd said it a few times before and I didn't really mean it. I didn't mean it then. I did mean it and I didn't, if you know what I mean."

Allen's creative crack-up turned into a classic Mexican stand off, with the band finally calling his bluff and accepting his resignation, thus plunging the keyboard player headfirst into a sea of self doubt. "We'd made it and I left the band. Instead of holding on a bit longer and sort of keeping myself quiet . . . actually to tell you the truth I shouldn't have left when I did because as you break the circle it starts going wrong. It's like a magic circle. I used to believe that."

Magic circles or just plain old crazy paving, Hunter for one was glad to see the back of the errant organist. Around the time of the Dudes tour, he had described Allen as a mixture of "hypochondriac, fanatic, self-dramatist . . . when he's down he's down, when he's up he's within reason . . . Phally's head is continually troubled and he has great difficulty in living, the reason being he wants everything right . . . he can storm out, grab you by the throat, be the most awkward bastard under the sun, but he's the most generous of us all."

By January, '73, Hunter had amended his assessment to the less complimentary, but more honest, rap that "he was a very intense, scary guy. We'd get into arguments, that kind of stuff. He had me by the throat more than once. I was scared of him."

Buffin, having known Allen from the early days back in Hereford, was a touch more diplomatic. "Why did he leave? In essence, because he had ceased to pull with the team and had, for some time, seemed to be an opposition force in the group. In no way did we ever think 'as one', but there had never been such a wide gulf in attitude within our ranks - and something, or someone, had to give."

With the troublesome Allen now well and truly out of the frame, the stage was set for Hunter, with Bowie's words still echoing in his ears, to exert a far greater influence on the group, without having to continually glance over his shoulder for that critical eye from behind the keyboard. It was Allen himself who had realised early on that "I was piggy in the middle with Ian and Mick when we were rehearsing. Buff was always reading (favourite print: *Superman* comics), and Pete would be there and they'd say; 'Have we got it together yet?' And I'd be saying to the other two; 'Oh, I'm not keen on this. I can't get off on this at all' . . . maybe I was the stabilising influence. Perhaps they didn't know that."

What they did know was that Allen's final vocal shot with the band, a song he had written himself called *Nightmare* and recorded prior to the AIR sessions at the new CBS studio (rated by Buffin as "awful") was shelved. Allen left London for Hereford and, with future Pretender Martin Chambers in tow, formed The Cheeks, a band destined to be consigned to endless trudging of the same pub and small club circuit that The Inmates had trodden almost ten years before. It seemed that Hunter's hour had finally arrived.

*"In the lyrics of the Mott album, I tried to get across that rock'n'roll isn't all superstars and God in the sky. There's losers and winners and varying degrees of losers and winners. It's honesty, really, Mott's a very honest band. Bowie was very dishonest but I still think he's incredible. I'm just saying; 'Wait a minute. This is how it really is."*

*IAN HUNTER.*

*"The songs ride the shuttle between introspection and gut blasting chord power and as you travel back and forth you realise that Mott The Hoople is the type of band that can be all things to all people - they're soft, they're loud, they're smart, they're dumb, sophisticated and punks, mods and rockers, geniuses."*
*BILLY ALTMAN / ZOO WORLD.*

## CHAPTER 14

**The album, simply titled *Mott*, was recorded over an eight week period commencing mid-February, 1973, at AIR Studio 2, although a couple of tracks (the aborted Hunter 'solo' efforts) were already in the can, the band having taped them at AIR 1 in January with engineer Alan 'Madswitcher' Harris. Housed in a lavish gatefold sleeve designed by CBS art director, Roslav Szaybo (in the States it sported a plain group pose photo), with a reprint of D.H. Lawrence's *A Sane Revolution* on the back, the songs, all carrying the 'arranged by Ian Hunter' tag, were in the main a reflection of the band's experiences during the U.S. leg of the Dudes tour. None more so than the record's kick off track, *All The Way From Memphis*, which opened with the line, "Forgot my six string razor and hit the sky / Half way to Memphis before I realised", a reference to a tantrum thrown by Verden Allen after a guitar he had brought in a pawn shop ("a little Ephiphone") was loaded onto the wrong plane.**

The song, originally titled *Rocker In C-Sharp*, was based on the band's final gig at the Ellis Auditorium (Hunter remembered that "we were headlining. The place was packed and the people were fantastic") which culminated in a wild after-gig party followed by a trip to Graceland which saw Hunter and Allen both slip past The King's hired muscle and, in Hunter's case, into the house. The droll lyric, with its potted history of music biz ups and downs, contained a note of caution to all would-be pop stars waiting in the wings, that "It's a mighty long way down rock'n'roll" and that it was not wise to be taken in by appearances in a game where "you look like a star, but you're still on the dole". Punctuated with a searing Ralphs' solo and old time doo-wop blowing from Roxy Music saxman, Andy Mackay (Hunter had bumped into Mackay backstage at Madison Square Gardens after Roxy had played a rather strained support slot to Jethro Tull. He was roped into the session after Hunter discovered Ferry and Co. recording their album, *For Your Pleasure*, next door), the song was an instant classic and, in an albeit edited form, extremely radio friendly.

Next up was *Whizz Kid*, Hunter's tale of a Manhattan hustlerette ("Little Whizz Kid mystified me / She was a New York City beat / She came on flash / Monster mash / Motors in her feet") with a chorus line lifted straight from the national anthem. The tune proved difficult to record, mainly due to its unusual arrangement, which led Buffin to believe that,

"Mick Ralphs hated *Whizz Kid* because he thought it was a rip off of a Free song called *Catch A Train*. Before it had a title for real, *Whizz Kid* was called *Catch A Cold*."

Hunter defended the track by admitting that "I only ever once forced a song on the group and that was *Whizz Kid*. The backtrack was very involved and sounded weird on its own. They were a bit worried then, but I could see the finished article." He went on to dismiss the guitarist's complaints, saying that "a song like *Whizz Kid* is very involved, and Ralphs couldn't understand why it had to be all over the place with these weird lyrics."

*Hymn For The Dudes* was a Hunter / Allen song which the recently departed organist had worked up "in 1971 sometime. We did it on stage before we recorded it in late '72". Originally little more than a jam, Hunter, inspired by their huge hit single, had added lyrics to Allen's cathedral like organ piece, encouraging the listener to immerse himself in the power of pop, but with a cautionary message not to take idols too seriously. Over a wailing vocal backing track provided by all girl back-up outfit The Thunderthighs (best known as the white girls who sang coloured on Lou Reed's *Walk On The Wild Side*), Hunter tore into the superficiality of superstardom, urging us not to be taken in by a bunch of young pretenders and to "Rejoice because The King ain't lost his throne / He's still here / And you are not alone", a calling card to those who, as he did, believed "passionately about young kids. They're amazing. They've got all the energy in the world. The song is just to say 'somebody cares about you' without sounding too corny (live it was coupled with Dylan's, *The Times They Are A Changing*). It's very hard to live at that age."

*Honaloochie Boogie*, the album's obvious single, was, according to Hunter "about being on the streets of Northampton with no money, and then someone turns you onto music", although the song's main source of inspiration turned out to be a David Essex movie. "I went to see *That'll Be The Day* and it reminded me of my days at the Town Hall dance, just waiting for a punch up." With Andy Mackay's gutterpunk saxophone and ex-Third Ear Band cellist, Paul Buckmaster's car chase style string arrangement, plus an infectious chorus repeated ad-infinitum into the fade (like *Dudes*), the song was picked up instantly by DJs, giving it a number 12 spot in the Top 40 by June, '73.

The side's closer, the hard hitting *Blackboard Jungle* dirty realism rocker, *Violence*, showed Hunter breaking free from some of his more predictable songwriting shackles and moving into an altogether tougher territory, the short, sharp shock administered in under five minutes. The song concerns an angry young working class boy ("I'm a missing link / Poolroom stink") trapped in a dead end existence ("Can't go to school / The teacher's a fool / The preacher's a jerk") whose only release from the urban hell of tower blocks and dole queues is the adrenalin rush of mindless violence ("It's the only thing that'll make you see sense") administered with random ferocity onto a faceless and uncaring society. Breaking off midway for a souped up simulated fight scene (inspired by an actual studio punch up between Hunter and Ralphs), and punctuated by an insane violin solo from Graham Preskitt, the song was as sharp as a blind alley switchblade. If anyone was in any doubt as to what it was like to be 14 and frustrated, then this song provided a clue. It hits you like a kneecap in the balls and hurts twice as much, and in a year when Mott's contemporaries from the late Sixties were still writing triple album "concepts" full of unintelligible lyrics and 15 minute organ solos, it showed a band out on a limb, ready to tell it like it really was. In 1973, only the Faces' rampant *Borstal Boy* came anywhere close.

Side 2 slides in with the Keith Richards' riff styled *Drivin Sister*, all about some hot rod mama who was "Rock'n'Roll / An automobeat on the street". On top of a greased up Ralphs' groove, Hunter sings a bunch of lyrics partly inspired by a madcap car journey with their creator. "Guy Stevens, our old manager, raced his VW through Hampstead Heath and Hyde Park," recalled Hunter, although it emerged that the problem was "he was driving it to the beat of a song from our first LP, *Half Moon Bay*. The song had at least ten time changes, and Guy raced the car to 70, then abruptly dropped it down to 10mph."

The song oozes speed and hairpin bends, but Buffin for one was disappointed with the end result. "*Drivin Sister* was a title nicked off The Stones. It's a total cock-up .It was meant to be a tough, raunchy track, and it ended up weedy and twee."

**MOTT THE HOOPLE**

the new album
**MOTT**

"Truly great albums aren't released every week - in fact I can only name six this year that fall into that category. Now here's the seventh, and I assure you it is the finest Mott the Hoople have done."
TONY STEWART, NME

"In short, this album marks a giant step forward for Mott; it should do very well." RF-C DISC

Honaloochie Boogie ● All The Way From Memphis
Whizz Kid ● Hymn For The Dudes ● Violence ● Drivin' Sister
Ballad of Mott The Hoople ● I'm A Cadillac
El Camino Dolo Rosa ●i Wish I Was Your Mother

CBS
the music people
on records and tapes.

Much sterner stuff followed with *The Ballad Of Mott*, a song credited to all the band (including, on the initial vinyl pressings, Verden Allen) and the elder brother of the shortly to follow *Saturday Gigs*, written in a Zürich hotel room on the 26th of March, 1972, after the band had decided to call it quits. The lyrics, penned in first person singular style, clearly belong to Hunter, as from the off he's confiding in us that he "Changed my name in search of fame / To find the midas touch / Oh I wish I'd never wanted then / What I want now twice as much". The tune was essentially written from a position of defeat and was obviously meant as a thank you to all the fans who had stuck with them as they "Crossed the mighty oceans / And we had a few divides", which tends to find it slightly miscast and sounding somewhat out of place (it makes a great B-side).

For band historians though, it serves as a vital document, telling in five minutes of the birth and (admittedly premature) death of a group in which "Buffin lost his childlike dreams and Mick lost his guitar / Verden grew a line or two and Overend's just a rock'n'roll star", before throwing a note of caution into the wind with "Rock'n'Roll's a loser's game / It mesmerises and I can't explain / The reasons for the sights and for the sounds". This was a song by a band who believed they had taken down the big top on the Rock'n'Roll Circus for the last time. Collectors will be interested in the fact that *The Ballad Of Mott* was included in the set for some of the shows on the Rock And Roll Circus Tour, and pops up on a bootleg of the band's Lyceum show of the 19th of April.

Mick Ralphs' only solo songwriting credit came in the shape of *I'm A Cadillac / El Comino Dolo Roso*, a motorvatin' woman as car metaphor, straight out of the Chuck Berry book of tunes, coupled with an achingly plaintive Spanish guitar drenched conversation piece. The track was an eight minute illegitimate offspring of a couple of studio jams, *No Jive* and *Elephants Gerald*, which served to slow things down dramatically, allowing the listener time to breath, before being taken by the hand and led into the album's closing ballad, the Hunter scripted, *I Wish I Was Your Mother*, in the eyes of many Mottphiles the shaded ones finest 4' 51" ever. A cautionary note to Trudi to keep an eye out for his ego ("Cos even if we make it / I'll be too far out to take it / You'll have to try and shake it from my head"), the band had originally wanted it as a single, even going as far as remixing it to 7" standard, but CBS, playing the corporate safety game, got cold feet and opted for the more upbeat *Memphis*, which justified its release by climbing to a respectable number ten that August. In the process though, it denied the single buying public one of the band's finest moments.

Left over from the sessions were *Rose* (a sensitive ballad about a "rock'n'roll slag" - surely a first - which made the flipside of *Honaloochie Boogie*), a 12 bar in E blues shuffle called *Where Do You All Come From*, plus a rough draft of a song the band would fiddle with on and off until summer, *Roll Away The Stone*, which was finally deemed presentable in June. Also at the studio around the same time was Verden Allen, although he managed to avoid the rest of the band. Buffin remembered him being "booked in Studio 1 with his band: Mick Jones (later of the Clash), Kelvin Blacklock, Jim Hiatt and an unknown bassist. Our spies reported that, after much huffing and puffing, the group began to play *No Wheels To Ride*. I went and had a listen through a 'secret' side door. It was truly appalling. Verden playing his Hammond sounded good, but the rest was dismal! After this session, which I guess was recorded, the producer who booked them in fired Mick Jones for 'being useless'. Even more fascinating is the identity of this benefactor of Verden Allen and chums. It was none other than his old adversary, Guy Stevens." (Trivia note: Jones and Blacklock, nicknamed 'Baby Jagger' because of his passing resemblance to the Stones' frontman, were fanatical followers of Mott and were known for spending many a night huddled together on freezing cold railway station benches after travelling miles to witness their heroes play in some provincial town hall. Many years later, following Hunter's departure, Blacklock actually got as far as auditioning for the job as lead singer).

In February, Mott had played a handful of northern dates as a four piece, supported by Scotland's soon to be sensational Alex Harvey Band, but it was obvious to all that their stage sound, now minus Allen's heavy driving Hammond, was nothing short of thin, and it was agreed that a replacement was needed before the forthcoming summer tour of the USA. So, in true Guy Stevens fashion, the band withdrew some money from petty cash, placed an ad in *Melody Maker*, then sat back to wait for the hopefuls to beat a path to their door.

*"It's funny really - we're neither big nor small in America. There's thousands that haven't heard of us but then again there's thousands that have. If you want a rough comparison I'd say we're about the same as The Velvet Underground were. Sort of a cult band. Now to be a cult band is great - our followers are fanatical in their support. I suppose that's why we're here. We've had enough messing about. It's time Mott started thinking about money. We won't be kids forever. Come on America, take us out of the cold. We're trying to catch you but you're so fuckin' big."*

IAN HUNTER.

*"I spotted another likely looking ad, which turned out to be Mott The Hoople. I went to the audition, and they seemed a very nice bunch of chaps, so I joined and found myself on a plane to America."*

MORGAN FISHER.

## CHAPTER

# 15

By the time he landed the gig with Mott, Morgan Fisher had travelled the yellow brick road from the depths of obscurity to the dizzy heights of teenybop stardom and back again to bottom of the bill gigs in half empty halls in countries not normally associated with scheduled stops on the rock'n'roll bandwagon.

Born in 1950, Fisher was musically inclined from an early age, and by the time he reached 15 he was a competent pianist. It was while attending Hendon Grammar school that he joined his first band, The Private Eyes, as a keyboard player. The band gigged intermittently on the local R&B circuit, but got no further than a name change to the more groovier sounding Beat Circuit before splitting after less than a year together, and in February, 1966, Fisher joined semi-pro act, The Soul Survivors, as organist. Managed by local businessman, Sidney Bacon, the group comprised of his son Maurice on drums, vocalist Steve Ellis, Warwick Rose on bass, and guitarist Ian Miller. The group proved to be a big hit on the home counties soul scene and even got as far as a gig at The Marquee before threatened legal action from a U.S. band with the same name (their *Expressway To Your Heart* on Stateside SS6158 was a big club hit in the summer of '67) forced a change of identity to the more poppier sounding Love Affair.

Signed by Decca, Love Affair, now consisting of Fisher plus Michael Jackson (bass), Georgie Michael (guitar), plus Bacon and Ellis, cut a version of The Stones' *She Smiled Sweetly* b/w *Satisfaction Guaranteed*, but the record, a weedy version of an album filler, bombed. Fisher, being something of a bright spark, then quit to take his 'A' Levels. In his absence, the group switched labels to CBS and, backed by a bunch of anonymous sessionmen under the guidance of future Womble, Mike Batt, recorded a version of Robert Knight's soul stomper, *Everlasting Love* b/w *Gone Are The Songs Of Yesterday*. When the song went stellar and hit number one, Fisher was hastily rehired to assist in the miming of the record for the Christmas edition of *Top Of The Pops*.

In April, *Rainbow Valley* b/w *Someone Like Me* hit number five, and the follow up, *A Day Without Love* b/w *I'm Happy* made number six. Even after the band came clean and admitted they hadn't played a note on their recordings, the singles still sold by the truckload, with both 1969's offerings, *One Road* b/w *Let Me Know*, and *Bringing On Back*

**Opposite page: Morgan Fisher (photo by Barry Plummer)**

*The Good Times* b/w *Another Day*, plus the album, *Everlasting Love Affair*, making the Top 20.

In March, 1969, Fisher played keyboards on Guns' *Gunsight* album and commenced playing live on stage with Love Affair, although the constant pressure of being teenybop idols finally got to Ellis, causing him to quit on Christmas Eve, 1969. He was swiftly replaced by Auguste Eadon, formerly of The Electric Band, and the group soldiered on, increasingly aware that their 15 minutes were fast running out. Sensing that their teenage audience were beginning to grow tired of them, the group changed their name to L.A. and recorded the album *A New Day*, but poor sales of this, plus the couple of singles lifted from it (*Lincoln County* b/w *Sea Of Tranquillity* and *Speak Of Peace Sing Of Joy* b/w *Brings My Whole World Tumbling Down*), prompted their label to drop them. Temporarily unemployed, Fisher accepted an offer to produce the band Igginbottom's one and only album, the now extremely rare, *Igginbottom's Wrench* (Deram SML1051). By January, 1971, L.A. had reverted back to their previous incarnation and had scored a deal with Parlophone, who released *Wake Me Up I Am Dreaming* b/w *That's My Name*, swiftly followed by *Help Me Get Some Help* b/w *Long Way Home*, but when neither single set the charts on fire they decided to call it quits.

In the summer of '71, Fisher formed Morgan, featuring himself plus Maurice Bacon on drums, Bob Sapsted on bass and Tim Staffel, recently departed from the band Smile, on guitar (which was probably a bad move on his part as within a year Smile had recruited bassist John Deacon along with enigmatic frontman Freddie Mercury and changed their name to Queen. More about them later). The group played their debut gig at The Marquee on the 3rd of September, 1971, and were quickly snapped up by RCA, although, much to their dismay, not by the London arm of the giant multinational. Instead the band travelled to Rome and inked a contract with the giant label's Mediterranean branch, who had designs on marketing them as a kind of Latin ELP. Desperate for a break, Fisher conceded to their wishes, resigning himself to the fact that "in Italy at the time there were lots of progressive rock bands. We were playing progressive rock, so it was easier to get a deal . . . "

The band spent the summer recording, and in December their debut album, *Nova Solis* (LISP34145), was released on the Continent, with about 500 copies (SF8321) trickling onto the U.K. market. The group gigged both home and away, but little success was forthcoming. Despite the setbacks, RCA indicated that they were interested in a follow up, and so in February, 1972, the band headed back to RCA's Rome studios, only to find a couple of weeks later that the label had had a change of heart and decided to put the project on hold (it was eventually released in the U.S. as *Brown Out* on Import Records IMP1006 and in the U.K. in 1979 on Cherry Red 1 as *The Sleeper Wakes*).

Back and broke in Blighty, Fisher moonlighted as a delivery driver for an off-licence, inbetween intermittent gigs with The Third Ear Band, until April, 1973, when he spotted the want-ad in the *Melody Maker* that would eventually lead him to Mott. Fisher recalled that "when I joined Mott there were two jobs going, one was as a piano player, the other as an organist (as well as replacing Allen, Hunter wanted to raise his frontman profile by moving out from behind the piano permanently . . . prior to the Dudes tour the group had always set up in a straight line across the stage, with Griffin's drums in the middle). I could have got either, but I took the job as pianist and I'm very glad I did."

The organist's stool was filled by the totally unknown Mick Bolton ("I didn't get the job because Morgan was a much better pianist. They gave me a job as an organist instead"), whose C.V. consisted of a stint in a couple of semi-pro acts, White Myth and Blind Eye.

The newcomers were initially put on wages with the understanding that the posts were on a trial basis only, and it was under this arrangement that they kicked off Mott's '73 U.S. tour in Chicago on the 27th of July, which, with the exception of a gig in Memphis on the 17th of August, concentrated entirely on the large industrial cities that made up the Eastern Seaboard. The band's original intention was to take a short break at the end of

August before hitting the all important West Coast in September.  But once again fate was to force their hand.

*"I'd been looking for an excuse to leave, I suppose. I'd been thinking about it for a long time. Since the band was becoming more and more Ian's thing, it just wasn't that musically satisfying for me anymore. I was getting frustrated because I'd been writing songs that weren't getting used in Mott. People said I was crazy to leave, because we were having such huge success, but I'd burned out on the band."*

*MICK RALPHS.*

*"Mars Bonfire. Fucking excellent name. Nearly as good as Ariel Bender, that guitarist from Mott The Hoople. I actually started writing a song called 'Ariel Bender'. It's that image of this guitarist, tight clothes, long hair and these little wrist bands . . . Ariel Bender. What a guy, man, he must have been ace."*

*NOEL GALLAGHER / OASIS.*

CHAPTER

# 16

Mick Ralphs, like Verden Allen before him, had become frustrated at not having his songs recorded by the band. Hunter's increasing dominance had meant that the guitarist, who once sang dual lead vocals and scored numerous songwriting credits, was now relegated to the Ringo of the group - one big song per album and maybe a couple of solo spots during the stage show - although Ralphs, who knew the band had suffered from a lack of direction in the past, grudgingly conceded that maybe Hunter was doing the right thing. "It was right for somebody to take control, but I did feel diminished. We were having success, so I wasn't gonna knock it, but I could see it was going to become Ian and the band. That irked me, I suppose."

That, coupled with the band's need to spend more time in the States which, to a nervous when airborn Ralphs meant daily flights, something he could only get through with a couple of stiff drinks and a handful of Mandrax.

Hunter had once described the frail guitarist as "your original loner. He'll run for miles to escape friendship when it's the one thing he needs. He campaigned to get out of the group flat, but having done so panicked." Hunter also acknowledged the debt the band owed Ralphs, saying that "he used to be our ace pusher, along with Guy Stevens, and he pushed Mott down the throat of Chris Blackwell. Mick was the kind of guy who, if you slammed a door in his face, would open it again smiling. He's now perplexed, uncertain and on the run all the time. His favourite answer is 'I don't know' - that's what the pressure does for you."

For some time, Ralphs had harboured an ambition to work with ex-Island stablemate, Paul Rodgers, who had gigged regularly with Mott over the years as both a member of Free and Peace, although the singer was amazed when Ralphs first ran the suggestion past him. "We talked about forming a group, but I said, 'No man, you can't leave that group. They're gonna be big'. It didn't seem to matter to Mick. He was more into what we were doing and so we did it."

"It" turned out to be Bad Company, a hard rock vehicle ready, willing and able to take on board the pile of songs that Mott wouldn't touch. Hunter, genuinely grieved at losing his old buddy, gracefully conceded that he had probably made the right decision.

"Mick played great on the (*Mott*) album, considering his heart wasn't really in it. But he really wanted to do something simple, and he later found the best person for that in Paul Rodgers. I don't blame him."

Mick Ralphs officially left the band on the 19th of August, 1973, after a gig in Washington D.C. As the tour schedule allowed only a three week break before the West Coast leg commenced, the group were faced with a real dilemma. Did they pull out of the tour, find a replacement, break him in gently and then try again in '74, or throw caution to the wind, grab whoever was available, and hope for the best? After much discussion between band, management, and promoters standing to lose thousands of dollars, the chips fell down in favour of option number two. After having spent the best part of four years trying to crack America, and with the *Mott* album picking up good vibrations, the group weren't about to blow it. Besides, Ian knew this geezer . . .

Mick Ralphs replacement was a guitarist who, rather ironically, he knew pretty well, both from the Guy Stevens days, and also because he had guested on his 1971 solo album, *Under Open Skies*. Luther Grosvenor was the man, and his form was as long as your right arm.

Grosvenor had made his professional debut in Deep Feeling, coming in as a replacement for the recently departed Dave Mason. The group, who also featured Jim Capaldi on vocals, Dave Meredith on bass, John Palmer on drums plus second guitarist Gordon Jackson, had started life as The Hellions before changing their name to Revolution. Their stint as Deep Feeling was to be short lived as Mason, who had teamed up with Steve Winwood, poached Capaldi for their new band, Traffic.

Grosvenor next surfaced in Carlisle band, The V.I.P's, who boasted Mike Harrison on vocals, bassist Greg Ridley, Mike Kellie on drums, and organist Keith Emerson. They had relocated to London where they came to the attention of Stevens who recorded them in 1966 (*I Wanna Be Free* b/w *Don't Let Go*) and 1967 (*Straight Down To The Bottom* b/w *In A Dream*) for Island, although the band's vinyl history stretched as far back as 1964 with RCA's, *Don't Keep Shouting At Me* b/w *She's So Good*. After Emerson quit to join The Nice, the band changed their name to Art, finding further work as the backing band on the Stevens' produced *Hapdash & The Coloured Coat* LP. They also cut another single for Island, a cover of Buffalo Springfield's *For What It's Worth / Rome Take Away Thee*, plus an album, *Supernatural Fairy Tales*, but following the recruitment of keyboard wizard Gary Wright, they opted for another name change, this time to Spooky Tooth, before proceeding to release albums and singles with alarming regularity. In October, 1971, Grosvenor recorded his solo album (featuring Ralphs on backing vocals) and, realising that Spooky were by now creatively bankrupt, jumped ship to join Stealers Wheel, where he stayed until July, 1973.

At home in Hampstead twiddling his thumbs ("I was out of work and lying in bed"), Grosvenor was surprised when, out of the blue, he got a call from Hunter offering him the guitarist's gig with Mott. He accepted immediately, but then found that contractual obligations with Mott's former employer, Chris Blackwell, necessitated the adoption of a nom-de-plume. It was singer / songwriter Lindsey de Paul, a friend of the band's and one time girlfriend of Buffin's, who chanced upon a suitably off the wall name, inspired in part by some nutter she had spotted outside a gig in Germany vandalising cars. From here on in, Mr. Grosvenor would be known to all and sundry as Ariel Bender. All the band, including their new recruit, were up for it, and within days Hunter was telling the *NME* that "I'm really excited because Ariel has this thing where he wants to be a rock'n'roll star and he wants to be noticed on stage and prance around and be a guitar hero. He's a great guitarist. He's gonna be great."

Thrown in at the deep end, Bender found himself with literally a couple of hours to learn the licks to Mott's new single, *All The Way From Memphis*, before making his debut on *Top Of The Pops*, miming to Mick Ralphs' studio track. He then flew to the States for a further 48 hours of intensive practice at Los Angeles' Aquarius Theatre before his American debut on the 13th of September edition of NBC TV's prestigious, *Midnight Special*. The band then kicked off part two of their tour on the 14th at the Hollywood Palladium, before hitting the road for a series of one nighters which took them all the way through to St. Louis on the 3rd of November. With their current album picking up encouraging reviews ("So well done and absorbing on every level . . . " - *Rolling Stone*, "Mott The Hoople are a great rock'n'roll band, dudes or no dudes". - *Zoo World*), the band found audiences more receptive than on previous excursions, and in many cities not before visited, they went down a storm. Their headline status now meant that they no longer had to taper shows to fit set support slot times, and their 90 minute set now ran as follows; *Drivin Sister*, *Sucker*, *Sweet Jane*, *Hymn For The Dudes*, *Walking With A Mountain* (re-introduced in favour of Mick Ralphs' *Ready For Love*), *All The Way From Memphis*, *Rose*, *All The Young Dudes*, *Jerkin Crocus*, *One Of The Boys*, *Rock'n'Roll Queen* and *Angeline*. At many of the shows, Hunter urged the audience to support Verden Allen's new band (although they never toured the States), but the spotlight was always on the new boy, whose heavy riffing and gaudy stage attire endeared him to mid-West audiences. By November, he was grudgingly admitting that "Ariel Bender is the perfect name for a guitar player".

**Above: Mott The Hoople (photo courtesy of CBS)**

The only sour notes from this otherwise trouble free leg of the tour was Hunter's arrest following a little post-gig argy bargy on the last day of October, resulting in a night spent at the Indianapolis City Jail, and on the 11th of November, when the band's Winterland concert was broadcast on West Coast radio. *Rolling Stone* magazine gave it a real pasting because, in their considered opinion, "the 'live' concert consisted of recorded versions of Mott's songs, all taken from their albums. These album cuts were sandwiched between a live recording of the band introducing their songs, and the audience reaction to those songs - with added crowd noise on top of this". The band countered by admitting that the magazine was correct, but that the broadcast was out of their hands, being part of a sponsorship deal they had at the time with Pioneer tapes.

Back home, the band barely had time to breath before hitting the U.K. concert circuit to promote their new 45, *Roll Away The Stone*, a song recorded earlier in the year with Mick Ralphs. The single, a catchy little Hunter homage to Fifties girl groups ("Sha la la la, push, push") with an extra large helping of Spector style bricklaying, was an instant hit in radioland, eventually climbing to number eight in the charts. Although it didn't score as high as Bowie's teen anthem, Hunter revealed later that the song was "the biggest selling single

I ever had. It was a lot bigger than *All The Young Dudes*. It came out in the middle of a huge rush and it sold an awful lot."

With headline status now permanently bestowed upon them both at home and abroad (CBS had released their singles throughout Europe, as well as in New Zealand and the Far East), the band had the power to call the shots concert wise. No more crappy village halls and converted gas holders, and never again any 20 minute, tenth on the bill slots at badly organised Stateside festivals. The support slot on the Stone tour was taken up by glam / pomp rockers Queen, who were at the time just beginning to make a name for themselves. Their manager Jack Nelson had secured their place by offering Bob Hirschmann £3,000 towards Mott's sound and lighting bill (standard practice even today), and, as eye witnesses revealed, they wasted no time in trying to upstage the headliners, although this rivalry helped to keep Mott on their toes. With Bender now adopting an increasingly up front and over the top role on stage, and in the process providing the perfect 'Keith' to Hunters strutting 'Mick', the band were now able to visually pack the same punch they had always pulled audibly. So much so that CBS decided to tape the final gig on the 14th of December at London's Hammersmith Odeon (two shows) for a prospective live album. The gig, which just happened to coincide with Buffin's wedding, was a stormer, garnering rave reviews in the music press. *Sounds'* columnist Martin Hayman summed it up perfectly, informing his readers that "Mott delivered a set brightened by the genuine rush of adrenalin inspired by a real near fist fight (the management tried to lower the safety curtain during the band's encore). Not all their gigs are musically superb, but this was real touch of the old Mott, the shambolic rabble-rousers. It's good that they're not falling into a cosy middle-age of success. It keeps you on the edge of your seat when you know such things can blow up at a moment's notice." And blow up they were about to.

*"I came from a different musical background, so when I started working with the group, it was different from just knowing the guys, different when you're working, business. We had great sessions, and the sessions were a bit up and down in the studio. One day a great session, another day it wouldn't happen. That applies to anybody."*

ARIEL BENDER.

*"He was fine at first because he copied Mick Ralphs' guitar parts, but when we got to do this album we found we had a lot of trouble with creativity."*

IAN HUNTER.

CHAPTER

# 17

After a short break for Christmas holidays, the band regrouped in January at Advision Studios to begin work on their next album which, before D.C. Thompson, publishers of *The Beano* got wind of it, had a working title of *The Bash Street Kids*. The original plan had been to record at Olympic with *Dudes'* engineer, Keith Harwood (they also tried engineer Bill Price at AIR, but at the time he was fully booked), but lack of investment meant that the studio was falling behind technically and the one track attempted, *The Golden Age Of Rock'n'Roll*, was scrapped. Further problems were awaiting at Advision when, just a couple of days into recording, house engineer Mike Dunne walked out, citing "creative differences" as his reason, although it is likely he was struggling to come to terms with the demands of a band under pressure to produce that all important killer album. His replacement was George Martin's right hand man at AIR, Alan 'Madswitcher' Harris, who had put some knob twiddling time in at the *Mott* sessions and was therefore hip to the band's style - although it appears that even he was second choice, the band having requested the services of Geoff Emerick, Martin's main man on dozens of Beatles' sessions.

With Hunter promising *Disc* magazine that "I want this one to be more aggressive than the rest", and with new boy Bender peeling off power chords to his heart's content, the band's sound underwent a dramatic change. The guitarist told the *NME* that "generally I played what I felt was right for the song. I played a lot of slide guitar, a lot of tremolo stuff. And on the whole I think the album is much stronger than what Mott have put out before." In the same interview Buffin revealed that "the songs are better. The arrangements are better. The recording's a lot better. We produced it ourselves. And we used an engineer called Bill Price whose absolutely amazing. Nobody seems to know about Bill Price. He's like a mystery figure. We don't really want to say too much about him, otherwise you get the Glyn Johns / Ken Scott touch where you have to talk to him through his manager!"

Some years later the drummer also sang the praises of another hero from the sessions, Alan Harris, saying that "he did the difficult bit . . . the awful sessions at Advision. Back at AIR, with Bill Price at the controls, we were horrified to find that the sounds on tape were not good. There were telephone calls between AIR and Advision. Machines were checked, test tones were consulted and the tension of the tape as it pressed the tape heads, the alignment of the tape heads checked. All to no avail. It still sounded dismal. We felt that it had been okay at Advision. At this point any other group would have scrapped the Advision tapes and re-recorded the lot at AIR with Bill Price. Mott The Hoople, however, were forced by management / record company to mix the album as it was."

Despite Bender's pronouncements regarding the extent of his input, it was clear to experienced ears that Hunter had arranged the songs heavily in favour of keyboards, a point highlighted by Morgan Fisher in an interview with *Sounds*. "Bender couldn't relax in the studio.  On Stage he was speedy too, four bars ahead of everybody.  Doing *The Hoople* album was quite tricky; we had to talk to him and encourage him a lot.  Bender was trying to adapt himself too much to the feel of the band, to replacing Ralphs, 'cos ya see Spooky Tooth was a very different band to Mott."

To make matters worse, Hunter chose to disappear to the States for a fortnight right in the middle of recording in order to sign the contracts for the publication of his forthcoming book, *Diary Of A Rock'n'Roll Star* - 159 pages of 'dear diary' style random thoughts and as it happens snapshots taken during the band's 1972 U.S. tour.- leaving the remaining members to "sort Bender out".  During this two week lay off, the band recorded Watts' *Born Late 58*, plus a couple of songs with a friend called Steve Hyams.  The line up for this session was Hyams on vocals, plus Buffin, Watts and Fisher, augmented by guitarist, Bruce Irvine (the songs taped at this particular session are not to be confused with those recorded by the band and Hyams in 1977).

Also present during the recording of *The Hoople* were former Dusty Springfield backing vocalists, Sue Glover, Sunny Leslie, Barry St. John and her husband, session saxophonist supreme, Howie Casey.  Also on hand were the ever faithful Graham Preskitt on orchestral arrangements, Lyndsey de Paul, long suffering Stan Tippins on back-up vocals, and Andy Mackay, who this time around was credited as Rockin' Jock McPherson, much to the displeasure of Mr. Casey, something of an icon on the saxophone scene.

Buffin disclosed that "Howie Casey wanted to be left off the credits . . . because he thought Andy Mackay was such a dreadful player that people might think it was Howie playing badly.  He was very upset." (Note for trivia buffs: Howie Casey's career began back in Liverpool with Howie & The Seniors, who were the first Liverpool band to get a recording contract.  Howie goes down in local folklore as being the man who, on hearing that The Beatles were to join his and a host of other bands in Germany, begged promoter Alan Williams to think twice because, in Howie's opinion, the soon to be biggest band in the history of recorded music were so bad that they would ruin a good thing for all the other Scouse rockers).

The finished album crashed in with the raucous *The Golden Age Of Rock'n'Roll*, with its doo-wop girlie lead in, spoken introduction (CBS exec Dan Loggins doing his best Alan Freed impression), and barrelhouse piano, climaxing into a crescendo of saxophones with Hunter ripping into the lyric at 100mph as if his life depended on it.  Buffin explained that "the lyrics are about the Leeds thing that keeps the volume down to 96 decibels.  Rock'n'roll is for the young and to be enjoyed, and now these old bastards are trying to cut it down.  The song is telling them to leave us alone."

The "Leeds thing" referred to a letter Hunter had received from a fan complaining about her local town hall's noise restriction policy at concerts.  Hunter put pen to paper and wrote to the council on her behalf, but all he received was some glib reply.  His anger at what he saw as nothing more than petty bureaucracy ("96 decibel freaks") became channelled into the song which, contrary to its title, was not some second hand nostalgia trip, but a celebration of here and now.  "If anything, the golden age of rock'n'roll has been in recent years," said Hunter, "where they tell me the industry has picked up phenomenally even without people like The Beatles."

Next up was Hunter's ode to rock star paranoia, *Marionette*, which was nothing short of a mini opera condensed into 5' 3".  Journalist John Tiven informed the readers of *Zoo World* (a major champion of the band in the U.S., along with *Fusion* and *Creem*) that the song "is prime sirloin, a vivid portrayal of the rock puppet, in mere minutes cutting to shreds Bowie's attempt on *Ziggy*.  Hunter succeeds because he's got not only starry eyes, he's got a rock'n'roll soul."  The author of this mini masterpiece told Radio 1 listeners that "this is all the band's favourite.  This is everybody's favourite that's heard the pressing so far . . . I believe it's the best track that Mott's ever done . . . it's something I've been wanting to do personally as a songwriter and that is to do a five minute opera as opposed to an opera that goes on for 40 minutes which I feel might be a bit trying . . . when I listen to music I like to hear a hitch all the time and I think we got it with *Marionette* and I think this is the first track we ever really got it all the way through . . . one thing hits you, another thing hits you, and you don't get room to sit back."

The song, with the standard Mott thumping piano, heavy duty riffing and a truly inspired call and response schoolyard bully of a chorus ("Marionette / I ain't one yet / Teacher's pet / Well you better forget it"), charts our hero's rise to the dizzy heights of axe wanker supreme, only to realise in the end that he's sacrificed every ounce of his integrity to get there ("He wanna play a riff to the man with the wires / He wanna play lead but his hands getting tired / He just wanna play but don't know how to say / STOP!"), and has ended up as little more than a puppet in the hands of record company grey men ("I gambled with my life / And now I've lost my will to fight / Oh God these wires are so tight"), finally forcing himself to come clean and admit that "I'm just a marionette".

*Alice* was an upbeat tale of a New York hustler ("She was a 42nd beat on 42nd Street") who had "golden ambitions and dead rhinestones on her feet" which reminded Hunter "of Manhattan / The seedy and the snazz / The shoeboys and the satins", although the babe's dreams of stardom were anchored firmly in the low rent end of Times Square ("It's a long way to Broadway for a 42nd lay / Or is it really just a couple of blocks away?"). Buffin remembered the song being heavily influenced by Nils Lofgren, and he said at the time that "Watts and I love his group Grin and stole the bass sound they use . . . we did credit them though." Close inspection of the lyric sheet indeed reveals the credit "Overend; Leslie Bass (thanks Grin!)." Nuff said.

The side closed with another social comment flame job in the same vein as *Violence*. *The Crash Street Kidds*, under its original title of *The Bash Street Kidds* was to have been the album's title track, but after problems with Thompsons it simply became the album's killer cut. Set in some nameless inner city hellhole, the protagonist, a very angry young man, urges us to "See my thoughts / See my scars / See my clothes / I dress to kill", before informing us that him and his boys are "coming to get you". The song oozes frustration ("Hear me swear / Hear every word / I ain't just a number / I wanna be heard") from a mind trapped in the living hell of tower blocks, dole queues and, a fair few years before The Sex Pistols, no future ("We'll torture your flats / You treat us like rats / Then you tell 'em we're brats / And the press twist our fist / Get me out of this mist"), which culminates in a burst of machine gun fire criss-crossing the speakers to the Dalek-like screams of "Now you're dead!". A few years later many punk rock bands cited Mott as a major influence, and if ever there was a song to make a 16 year old social outcast pick up a guitar and tell it like it really is then this is it. Malcolm MacLaren may have thought he invented punk, but Ian Hunter, no stranger to a little argy-bargy himself, was years before his time. For a band trying hard to court a Top 20 audience, this song was a very brave move indeed, and over 20 years later, the issues it raises are still with us.

In an interview broadcast in February on Radio 1, Hunter told the BBC's Michael Wale that he'd "got this preoccupation that when you go to new towns they don't seem to have any centres in them. Where I was brought up you always had a centre where you could go and there was a lot of people walking round and they frightened me to death, and I mean, that's the way we're going. This is the story of a street gang in one of these towns that are getting pretty fed up by the monstrous way things are run in this country at local government and national government level and they decide they're gonna take over, they're gonna take over Britain."

Hunter then went on to introduce Side 2's opening shot, *Born Late 58*, explaining that "this is the first track that we've ever done by Overend Watts . . . I went away for a week and when I came back it was done and I couldn't believe it. I mean I think it's a single. For a guy to come in and put his first song to the group, which it was, it was the first song he'd ever put to the group. I just couldn't believe how good it was. I was sort of mentally preparing myself to say 'Look, well you know, Pete', but it's great. It just knocks me out. I find myself putting it on all the time."

With its false start (turn the volume up and you'll hear the cry for "More treble, this is Manfred Mann's bass!") kicking into a crunching riff (Watts on Rickenbacker 12 string), with the killer opening line about how "Baby took me out last night / Got a little Cadillac bite / She shook me about - inside out / Didn't get home 'til light", the song careers across the highway like a juggernaut out of control (Bender's slide solo is all over the asphalt) as Watts lays it on the line about the perils of underage sex (at the time of the album's release any girl born in 1958 would have probably been a few months shy of the legal limit) and how you can "Create her, mistreat her / No use trying to beat her / Admit it, she's greater / Shame you weren't born later".  Powered along by Fisher's Jerry Lee Lewis on speed piano, and Griffin's phased out drumming, the song was an instant hit with listeners everywhere, and was destined to be a feature of future live shows, much to the delight of those fans fed up with reading about how Watts and Co. were nothing more than Hunter's backing band.

*Trudi's Song* slowed down the proceedings considerably, Hunter describing the sensitive ode to his wife as being influenced by his old idol, Bob Dylan.  "A lot of people didn't like *Nashville Skyline*, but I liked *Nashville Skyline*, especially the vocal sound, the way it came out of the speakers and from the production point of view.  I thought we got a good vocal sound on it.  Morgan Fisher plays excellent piano (major use of the trusty old Leslie cabinet, Verden Allen's old ace up the sleeve) . . . he's playing like he's been with us since the beginning."

*Pearl 'n' Roy (England)* got things back on the political track, with the faded in "Cosh & Helmet" bar room scene giving Hunter a platform to vent his spleen about the boys and girls who made up the Seventies social hierarchy while the rest of us were left to "Clean the chimneys kids 'cos it's 1974 / Shake a fist, make Oliver Twist / There's no way you ain't poor".  The song was written at the height of political and social unrest ("The uni-own jack is starting to crack / The greed breeds killing off the grass"), but quickly dated following the general election and a change of government.  Even so *Pearl 'n' Roy* (originally titled *J.C's Alright*) was as sharp a piece of political satire you were likely to hear outside of a northern workingmen's club, and a testament to Hunter's uncanny ability to put his finger on the working class button and avoid, as many rock stars fail to do, sounding patronising.

After taking the mickey out of the upper crust, Hunter then turned around and did it to himself.  *Through The Looking Glass*, a beautifully orchestrated piece (take a bow, Graham Preskitt) chronicling the every day existence of your average rock star ("Feeling ugly, feeling low, morning mirror, I ain't no rose"), the primping and pruning, the posing and the paranoia ("Do you have to paint teeth green, when they're snowy white and clean / Do you have to make eyes red , make them clear and fresh instead") and the in-built capacity to self destruct at the drop of a hat ("I'll never look at you again / Cos I'm really not that vain / Seven years bad luck ain't too long / But before I smash you, hear this song").  In *Through The Looking Glass*, Hunter was willing to admit what many others were only too eager to deny - that rock'n'roll is all about illusion and nothing is ever what it seems.  From the poser who "looks like a star but is still on the dole" in *All The Way From Memphis*, to the motormouthed gang leader in *The Golden Age Of Rock'n'Roll* who knows that "you've gotta be young man, you can never grow old", the message is pure and simple.  Love it, loath it, but don't ever let it take you in.  (Note: an alternate vocal of this song was recorded, featuring Hunter hurling a torrent of expletives at Dan Loggins, who was in the control room at the time).

The album closes on a light hearted note with a re-recorded run through, *Roll Away The Stone*, with Ariel Bender playing the part of Mick Ralphs, and Lyndsey de Paul doing her best to sweet talk Hunter during the break.  Also cut at the sessions were *Rest In Peace*, a Hunter / Watts / Griffin composition in the same vein lyrically as *The Ballad Of Mott* and *Foxy Foxy*, a cute little Hunter homage to Phil Spector's girlie groups.

Released on the 22nd of March, the album proved to be both a critical and commercial success, making number 11 in the U.K., and a respectable 28 in the U.S. where, to be fair, it was competing against the *Rock'n'Roll Queen* compilation, which Atlantic finally got around to releasing that summer, scoring a 112 chart placing.  Although

*The Golden Age Of Rock'n'Roll* 45 only managed a 96 position on the Billboard chart (it hit number 16 at home), the band were now classed as a major concert attraction, and plans were formulated for their biggest assault yet on the American gig circuit.

Meanwhile, back in Britain, a short tour was quickly thrown together to push the album in the provinces. On the 20th of March, the band appeared on *Top Of The Pops* to plug their latest single, and the following night, accompanied by solo support act Judi Pulver, they hit the motorways for seven nights, criss-crossing the country to play shows in Bradford, Leicester, Bristol, Sheffield, Paignton and Bournemouth.

# The Story of Cinder Hoople
### (A tale of rock 'n' roll glitz and glamour)

Once upon a time, in a far out land, there lived a young waif named Cinder Hoople.

Cinder Hoople was always sad because her wicked stepmother and ugly stepsisters never let her wear platform shoes. Or glittery make-up. Or spangled T-Shirts. Or even funky dresses. In short, they wouldn't let her be the outrageous creature she knew she was.

One day a proclamation was read throughout the land: "Free rock concert! Everyone invited!" Cinder Hoople begged her wicked stepmother to let her buy a new outfit for it. Alas, "No," was her reply.

On the night of the concert, a vision appeared to the weeping Cinder Hoople.

"Hark! I am your fairy godmother."

"Don't hark me," said Cinder Hoople. "I've got troubles of my own. I've got nothing to wear to the concert."

"No sweat, sweetie," said the fairy godmother and with a flick of her wand, Cinder Hoople's plain duds were changed to the most faded of jeans, the most sequined of shoes and the greenest of nails.

"What a far-out fairy," said Cinder Hoople. The rest is history. The prince of rock found the glass platform Cinder Hoople lost while fleeing the concert after the riot. He whisked her away to his suite at the Holiday Inn where she was crowned Rock 'n' Roll Queen and they made beautiful music together ever after.

**MOTT THE HOOPLE ROCK AND ROLL QUEEN**

"Rock 'n' Roll Queen" from Mott The Hoople. Eight of their best songs on one fabulous record. On Atlantic Records and Tapes.

Produced by Guy Stevens, Shadow Morton and Mott the Hoople

Although it initially appeared that everything was hunky dory within the group, later evidence indicates the contrary. Ian Hunter revealed that "it sounds like I was given too much room. It's overblown. It sounds like Ralphs isn't there, and I'm trying to overcompensate", while Buffin, now a major player in the production stakes, admitted that "I probably sat on *The Hoople* more than anyone else. It was a ghastly experience. Wrong studio (Advision), wrong engineer (Bill Price / Geoff Emerick unavailable), country in crisis, strikes, electricity cut offs, petrol shortage, etc., Bender, not enough songs (unlike every previous album, there was nothing left over from these sessions). During the Advision sessions the engineer 'had a nervous breakdown' and was never seen again. Hunter disappeared, for no apparent reason to New York, and Watts, Fisher and I were left to 'sort Bender out'. Not possible. Ian was furious when he got back . . . "

Finally, to add insult to injury, Morgan Fisher's portrait was omitted from the front cover collage of the album sleeve (once again designed by Szaybo), because CBS reckoned he was still technically under contract to RCA and, in an attempt to avoid any legal hassles, they preferred to foster the illusion that he was just a hired session player.

On the 7th of April, the band flew to Los Angeles for a couple of days' rehearsals before hitting the road in Phoenix on the 11th on a tour that would take them across the country and into Canada, culminating in a final show in Ontario on the 28th of May. For the duration of this trip they took along organist Blue Weaver, a veteran session player who had also gigged with Amen Corner and The Strawbs. Weaver replaced Mick Bolton, who at the time was said to have left for "religious reasons" (he had designs on becoming a Jehova's Witness), although it is more likely that the band just didn't get on with him. Some years later, Buffin threw a little more light on the situation when he said that "he surfaced in the early Eighties, having won a competition for 'best pub pianist' in London or England. We'd not seen him since the time he'd left Mott - when he turned up at Watts' house with a cassette full of (O.K.) demos. Nothing spectacular, though. He's a very nice chap - but, as before, his wife caused a terrible scene and embarrassed him and everybody else. We've not seen or heard of him since."

Bolton's replacement, according to Hunter, was brought in "on impulse. He was in the studio one day. Morgan knew him from his teenybop days. He was around doing nothing so we thought 'why not?'. We knew he had the ability to do what's necessary."

Weaver himself remembered being "absolutely skint. I was mini-cabbing and washing dishes and I didn't even have a keyboard or equipment. I began to hang around studios to see if there was any work going and one day I ran into Morgan Fisher . . . he told me that Mott just decided to get a new keyboard player . . . and within minutes I was in the band."

The challenge now was to crack the States wide open. The record sales were healthy, the audiences were out there, and the band were fired up artistically. The jackpot was finally within reach.

*"In the climb to success, Mott The Hoople has left behind a trail of disgruntled managers, producers and group members, as well as their most convincing music. Classic hard rock is anarchic in nature, and early MTH played with a conviction that only comes to lower middle class rock musicians who know if the group doesn't make it, it's back to the coal mines."*

*CRAWDADDY / JULY '74.*

*"Success didn't change the group - but it did have a big effect on those around it."*

*BUFFIN.*

## CHAPTER

# 18

Mott kicked off their '74 assault in Uncle Sam's backyard at the Celebrity Theatre in downtown Phoenix on the 11th of April. With them for a good portion of the tour were Queen, making their U.S. debut (their *Now I'm Here* 45, released at the end of the year, was about their experiences supporting Mott), although other acts opening during the latter stages included Aerosmith, Blue Oyster Cult, Z.Z. Top, Dr. Hook, Kansas, The Pointer Sisters plus the enfant terribles of the Stateside glam scene, The New York Dolls. Mott themselves had tried hard to shrug off the glam tag, but their connection with Bowie, at least in the eyes of the American public, meant that they were occasionally lumped in with what by mid-74 was becoming a dying fad, particularly in the States where, outside of the major coastal cities, it had never been that big a deal in the first place.

For this run of shows the band had tightened up the changes, introduced extra lighting, and broadened the set list, which now ran as follows; Intro (*American Pie*), *The Golden Age Of Rock'n'Roll*, *Sucker*, *Roll Away The Stone*, *Sweet Jane*, *Rest In Peace*, *Here Comes The Queen* (a song from Bender's solo album, performed by the guitarist), *One Of The Boys*, *Born Late 58*, *Hymn For The Dudes*, *Marionette*, *Drivin Sister*, *The Crash Street Kidds*, *Violence*, *All The Way From Memphis*, *All The Young Dudes* and *Walking With A Mountain*. On the 12th and 13th of April, the band performed at The Santa Monica Civic Auditorium, with the second of these shows being aired live on many syndicated West Coast radio stations. Needless to say the broadcast later emerged as a bootleg known as *Rest In Peace*. Other illegal platters culled from this show include *The Golden Age Of Mott The Hoople* and *Behind Enemy Lines*.

The tour wound its way through the Southern states, hitting Kansas City, St. Louis, Oklahoma City, Memphis and New Orleans (all Mott strongholds), before a seven day layover in New York City for what was to be the highlight of the tour, a week's worth of shows at The Uris Theatre and the distinction of being the first rock band ever to perform on Broadway. The coup was down to the sharp operating of the band's New York based manager, Fred Heller, who, along with his U.K. counterpart Bob Hirschman (H & H Management), had pulled out all the stops to make sure his boys received a high profile wherever they went. It was just like the days of MainMan and Tony de Fries, only this time the band had the billing and record sales to back the flash up.

Good though he was at his job, Heller wasn't everybody's favourite person. "The guy was an egotistical jerk who was only interested in Ian," reckons Morgan Fisher. "He considered the rest of the band to be completely dispensable. I remember once when Buffin complained about something one night, he said to Buffin, 'What else would you do if you weren't in Mott - pump gas?'. One of the most despicable people I have ever worked with."

**Opposite page: Buffin (photo by Barry Plummer)**

The New York shows were a triumph (the band were joined on stage by The Pickwick Puppet Theatre during *Marionette*), with a total of seven shows being played in all (the 12th of May date, which was strictly optional, was cancelled), with rave reviews in the press and ecstatic scenes in the audience (future Bon Jovi guitarist Richie Sambora remembers going to see Mott and Queen three nights on the trot and being totally blown away each time). Bob Edmonds, writing in *Creem*, said that "to my way of thinking there could've been no better band to open up Broadway's belly than Mott The Hoople. They've earned the right to that much frosting on the cake with five years of diligently rendered service. And they further earned it by virtue of the fact that they could look all the pomp and circumstance full in the face and still giggle about it over in the corner: 'Is that really us?'"

Morgan Fisher recalls shooting a film that was shown at some U.S. concerts. "It was just a film I made on tour. Mott The Hoople and Queen. It was just life on the road. Like a holiday movie or a home movie. Basically, I shot it when we were travelling, going to hotels and restaurants . . . it was Queen's first American tour. But it was not so much about Mott or Queen. It was mostly about things we saw in America when we were travelling on the road . . . "

But it wasn't all rave reviews and critical plaudits. In his definitive book on Led Zeppelin called *Hammer Of The Gods*, author Stephen Davis recounted an embarrassing celebrity incident involving the Zep's sticksman John Bonham that wouldn't have appeared out of place in the spoof rock'n'roll movie, *This Is Spinal Tap*. Davis recalled that "after the party Bonzo kept drinking. That night he blundered backstage at the Uris Theatre on 54th Street, where Mott The Hoople was playing. Bonzo wanted to sit in on drums and jam, and was told to piss off, no arrangements had been made . . . Mott's crew thumped Bonzo soundly and threw him out of the theatre on his arse." The crew in question were tour manager Stan Tippens, plus roadies Richard Anderson and Phil John, who had all been with the band from day one. Also on hand was soundman Mick Hince, who joined the ranks on the Mott tour, plus former Bowie sidemen Leee Black Childers (assistant road manager) and Bob Coffee (a.k.a. Bob 'C', sound technician), who had both worked with the band on the '72 Dudes excursion.

The group's show had now become a grandiose affair with Hunter in particular playing the rock icon role to the hilt. He was ably assisted in all areas by Bender whose power chord riffing and strangled solos went down well with audiences raised on home grown axe heroes like Joe Walsh and Ted Nugent. Bender went on record as saying that "I know I played a big part in Mott's image in America", but to many ears back home something was missing. Sure, the shows were lively affairs, well played and choreographed to the hilt, but, as the numerous bootlegs from the tour indicate, there was one essential ingredient missing from the equation. A couple of years earlier, Hunter had suggested that David Bowie's shows had lacked humanity. To many who had witnessed the band in their wild 'n' free Island days, it seemed that they were now heading down the same highway. Hunter had now adopted the role of the ringmaster (his sexist banter during *Angeline* was dodgy even by '74 standards - today it is nothing short of embarrassing), while Bender, playing the axe hero, had substituted the understated solos of Mick Ralphs with a raging torrent of sub-heavy metal riffs played with minimum finesse at maximum volume. Many die-hard fans blamed the introduction of Bender into the fold for the sudden increase of style over substance, but the guitarist defended himself by saying that "they (the band) would never demand me to do anything, but I found myself becoming a different player to what I really am."

Hunter's profile had increased considerably of late, due in no small part to the publication of his book, *Diary Of A Rock'n'Roll Star* (published as *Reflections . . .* in the U.S., although at one point it was going to be called *Rock'n'Roll Sweepstakes*, a title its author vetoed - he wanted to call it, *I'm A Mug!*). As a sweetener, extracts had been published in the *NME* back home and in *Creem* in America, and the book was hailed by fans and critics alike as a minor masterpiece. As a rock music document it makes for essential reading, telling as it does exactly what it's like to be a member of a band, not too big but not too small, working hard to crack the American market. Hunter prefaces the book by writing: "This is a documentary about a band I'm in . . . It was written as it happened, on planes, buses, in cars, hotels, dressing rooms - anywhere I could put pen to paper. Sometimes I was tired, sometimes drunk, sometimes corny high and sometimes very down . . . It's not meant to have literary merit, nor to be a journalist's delight. No, it's more like a letter to a fan in the front row of the Rainbow, a diary to keep in touch. It's meant as a buzz for the people who dig us and will never be able to go to the places we travel. I hope the kids we play to will read it and that it will give them some pleasure."

Exactly 20 years later, music critic Stuart Maconie, writing in Q magazine, gave the book a long overdue reappraisal, coming to the conclusion that it was "the greatest rock book ever written". His article is re-produced below courtesy of Q.

"There have been bigger rock stars than Ian Hunter; there have been deeper thinkers, and there have certainly been prose stylists with more éclat, but none of them have emulated this little book's piercing insight, pace and robust good humour. Every page has the salty tang of real life and a particularly odd brand of real life at that. The book covers Mott's five-week U.S. tour in November and December, 1972. The timing is crucial. Glam and prog rock rule and records sell in quantities undreamed of now. Furthermore, political correctness is a long way off. Herewith, Hunter on groupies: 'They're lousy lays and as a rule you can never get rid of them once you've let them in. They don't even listen to the music anymore and you run a big risk in the dose stakes if you decide to dabble. The best thing to do, young and inexperienced, is to whip their spotty little arses, lay back and enjoy a professional blow job, then tell them you've got crabs and they'll be gone before you know it'. There's a healthy amount of this. 'Birds', 'booze' and coarse language abound. But Hunter is never boorish. He could self-deprecate for England and is almost courtly in his dealings with other musicians. Certain themes recur. Hunter's beer gut, Mick Ralphs' fear of flying, the quest for cheap guitars. Zappa, Bowie, Keith Moon and others flit in and out. Hunter gets drunk a lot and moans about hotels, journalists and hangers-on. He is ludicrously informative in a chummy off the cuff way about riders, hotels, promoters, plane travel and how to buy cigarettes in America. Intending the book as a 'letter to the fan in the front row of the Rainbow', he relates everything to the lifestyle of 'the kid in Sheffield or Newcastle whose only buzz is signing on twice a week'. Hunter's personality is Haight Ashbury out of the taprooms of his native Shropshire and the result is a big hearted, cheeky, roast beef-and-two-veg pop picaresque. Suspicious of everyone, trying to buy the Daily Mirror, looking out for the Hereford United result, and eating shepherds pie every night with the whole cuisine of New York at his disposal, he is side-splittingly British. It's a three-day-week and Love Thy Neighbour inflected view of the rock biz. And it succeeds better than anything before or since."

Maconie is spot on regarding Hunter's writing style, although he does exaggerate certain points. Hunter only mentions The Daily Mirror and Hereford United once (and not in the same context - as Q pointed out in 1996, Hunter actually supports Shrewsbury Town!), he only eats shepherds pie twice (at The Haymarket on 8th Avenue . . . his obsession with weight marks him down as a salad man) and the booze consumption, compared to many rock'n'roll bands, is positively monastic. What the book does bring across is the unrelenting tedium of travelling (mostly planes, with the odd Greyhound ride thrown in for good measure), the boredom of endless soundchecks (constant arguments over who goes first), the dodginess of the promoters (cancelled gigs and backstage rows) and the sheer exhaustion of trying to look like a star from morning to night, which Hunter dismisses by saying that "anybody who thinks musicians work barely an hour a day is a mug. I've worked 16 hours a day for Mott since Mott's creation . . . attitude is a big word if you REALLY want to make it. In a group you're a diplomat, nurse, confidant, taxi driver, labourer, electrician, tailor, designer, and a few other things I can't mention, before you even get on stage."

The tour wound up in Richmond, Virginia, on the 2nd of June, and the following day the band travelled up to New York to catch a plane back to London. In his Dobbs Ferry offices, Fred Heller was already pencilling in dates for an April through to June '75 U.S. tour, including several nights at Madison Square Gardens, while over in London a major U.K. tour between the 10th of November and the 20th of December had already been finalised. All the band needed now was a couple more hits to promote.

*"Elvis Presley Boulevard. Wonder if they'll ever have Hunter Terrace or something like that in Wembley?"*

*IAN HUNTER.*

*"We were simple people. Just ordinary English drunkards. We just enjoyed. We had many parties. Everybody said that Mott The Hoople was a great party band because after every concert we had big parties in the hotel."*

*MORGAN FISHER.*

## CHAPTER

# 19

Within days of returning from the gruelling American trek, the band were in the *Top Of The Pops* studio taping a slot for their new single *Foxy Foxy* (Hunter reckoned that it was "the only thing I've ever done with Mott that I didn't really mean . . . 'cos I wrote that for Ronnie Spector, and we were supposed to meet her in New York when we were doing Broadway, but she never showed up"), before hitting the road again to play a handful of open air gigs, most notably the Buxton Festival in Derbyshire and the Isle Of Man's Palace Lido.

Since the *Dudes* album, CBS had been issuing the bands LPs as well as the odd single in Japan (Island released the *Rock'n'Roll Queen* compilation in Japan, and Sony issued *All The Young Dudes*, *One Of The Boys*, and *Roll Away The Stone* as 45s - albeit in EP form with other artists - in Thailand). It was therefore no surprise to find the band looking eastwards in search of new markets, particularly since outside of a couple of European strongholds and the good old U.S. of A., they had never trodden the boards in other territories. Buffin recalled that "plans to tour Japan / Australia in 1974 was very serious. An offer was made for us to tour - all expenses paid but no fees. Due to the high cost ofgoing south of the equator, we thought this a good promotional idea to give us a chance to break those areas. But our management refused, and Queen took up the offer."

Instead the drummer took to the mixing desk with tapes from the '73 Hammersmith gig and a radio broadcast from one of the Uris shows (part of the deal in allowing the gig to be broadcast was that the band got the tapes to use as a live album, a real cheap shot from CBS who showed no interest in investing in high quality equipment in order to record all seven shows and then edit down the best tracks) with instructions to come up with a live album as quickly as possible, to coincide with the bands next U.K. tour, which was scheduled to kick off on the 10th of November at the Glasgow Apollo. As if that wasn't enough, the band were booked on to a European tour, beginning in Sweden in early October.

What with the *Foxy Foxy* single performing well below everyone's expectations (it only made number 33) and the obvious lack of decent raw material for the forthcoming live album (plus a chronic shortage of material in the can), it was inevitable that tensions were running high, and it was no surprise to find Bender being offered up as the whipping boy. Things came to a head when the band attempted to record a rough draft of a Hunter song called *Saturday Kids*. Buffin recalls that "the guitar solo . . . was his last chance. He blew it!"

It was officially announced that Bender had quit to form Widowmaker with former Love Affair vocalist Steve Ellis, but to anyone prepared to look between the (head)lines, it was obvious that he had been sacked. Morgan Fisher, who had himself recently dabbled in a couple of outside projects (in November, '73, he guested on Keef Hartley's *Lancashire Hustler* LP and the following September he recorded in Nashville with ex-Spooky Tooth member Mike Harrison on sessions for his *Rainbow Rider* album), who summed up the enigma that was Bender most eloquently. He said that the errant guitarist "was amazing on stage and became quite a well loved figure in the States. He was pretty much out of control. But let's face it, out of controlness these days seems to be looked on as something good, while in those days it wasn't, because things were getting very American. It was pre-punk, and it was when things were heading towards pub rock and all that sort of thing, and everyone was trying to get very slick. Ian was particularly influenced by America, things like Bruce Springsteen and all that, so eventually he decided - it was basically his decision - that Bender couldn't cut it as a guitarist. We couldn't find a way to harness Bender's energy, couldn't control it. It's a shame. We felt we had to control it, but that's the way it went . . . "

Hunter, on the other hand, was slightly more succinct, revealing that "Luther was real upset, and I was too. It's impossible to not love the guy. But it had to be done."

Bender, who Hunter had originally seen as encapsulating the primitive energy that had always been Mott's trademark live, was now being thrown out because Hunter didn't like his playing style. The singer added that, "some people thought he was better than Mick live. We had a lot of fun, and morale was never higher, but I knew it wasn't the same."

Buffin was also full of praise for the wild man, acknowledging that "for whatever reason, probably because the music was wrong for him, Luther never found his feet musically within the confines of Mott The Hoople. He worked hard, very hard though, and was a tremendous character to have around."

Morgan Fisher probably came closest to the truth when he said, "There are some musicians who can perform well in many different situations; others need the right blend of musicians around them - Ariel was the latter breed, I think. That combined with the pressure of Mott finally making it, with all that that involves, made it hard for him. He compensated very well by being visually stunning on stage."

The guitarist himself remained philosophical, informing the music press that "I've had a great year with the band. I enjoyed it and I think it's time for me to do my own thing 'cos I feel it's the right time and I want to do it. It wasn't an easy decision."

It was clear that even though he had effectively been dumped by Hunter, Bender was still maintaining that he had jumped and had not been pushed, claiming that "after we finished the last American tour I made the decision to leave the band because I thought I could go out on my own. It's a big challenge." Considering that Bender was quickly absorbed into the ranks of another band (Widowmaker) the line about going "out on my own" seems a trifle hollow, although egos being what they are in the rock world, it was obvious that nobody wanted to lose face.

With the live tapes now mixed and ready for release, and with the European dates looming on the horizon, the race was once more on to find another guitarist, and although the names of Nils Lofgren (Buffin said that "Watts and I loved his group Grin . . . Nils turned up at the Washington show and met us backstage . . . great bloke") and Ray Major (a hot young guitarist from the group Hackensack who Mott had been eyeing up around the time of Mick Ralphs' departure), it was former Bowie sideman Mick Ronson, at the time struggling to make it as a solo artist, who finally got the nod, much to the dismay of Buffin who remembered that "no one was auditioned to replace Bender - we had decided to call it a day 'for the time being' when the name of Ronson came up and Ian was VERY enthused. Watts and I were less happy, because it meant 'getting into bed' with Tony de Fries, MainMan and all the attendant high pressure nonsense again. We'd had nine months of that in 1972 - it was quite sufficient."

*"I knew Ronson would argue with me. I respected him, I wouldn't get my own way all the time, and that's what I needed."*
                                        *IAN HUNTER.*

*"It was the dream that instantly became the nightmare - the one where everything goes horribly wrong and you are powerless to retrieve the situation - we were the spectres at our own feast."*
                                        *BUFFIN.*

## CHAPTER
# 20

Once again the band had been forced into making a snap decision regarding a guitarist, and once again it would be a decision they would all (with the possible exception of Hunter) live to regret.

Michael Ronson was born on the 26th of May, 1946, in Hull. As a child he showed considerable musical prowess, mastering the piano, violin, recorder and harmonium (in the local Mormon church) before he was in his teens. But it was as a guitarist that young Michael first made a name for himself, making his stage debut in a local group called The Mariners, who first dipped their toes in the rock'n'roll swimming pool supporting The Keith Herd Band (formerly Keith Kelly & The Crowd) at Elloughton village hall. Band leader Herd remembered that "Mick was very young - no more than 16 or so - and very nervous. He'd only been playing guitar for a very short time, and I'm pretty sure that Elloughton was his first public appearance. I gave him a few pointers on the guitar that night, but within a week or two he was already ahead of me."

Ronson told *Circus* magazine ten years later that "it was a pretty bad period for us. Most bands that were starving used to have to eat oatmeal dinners to stay alive. Sometimes we didn't even eat at all. I remember that at one point I used to eat four slices of dry bread a day. And when I got rich I used to eat a ham sandwich!"

After The Mariners dissolved, Ronson joined The King Bees (not to be confused with future employer David Bowie's band of the same name), who quickly mutated into The Crestas. Deciding to cast fate to the wind, the young guitarist opted to head for London to try his luck with the capital's burgeoning blues scene. Taking a part time job as a garage mechanic, Ronson soon found a home for his Jeff Beck influenced style in an R&B act called The Voice, although this soon fell apart when Ronson discovered that the band were financed in part by a quasi-religious sect called The Process, something he found at odds with his Mormon faith. A stint with soul group Wanted proved fruitless, and before long the young guitarist was heading back to Hull, where he was promptly snapped up by local hotshots, The Rats.

Ronson took a job in a local paint factory to supplement his meagre earnings, but was forced to quit his mundane day job when the group were offered a stint at The Marquee's sister club, The Golfe Drouot in Paris, during May, 1967. "Even then", recalled future Spider Trevor Bolder (then resident in rival Hull act The Chicago Style Blues Band), "he was known as the best guitar player in town. People would go to gigs just to watch him play: he was doing stuff on the guitar that no one else in town could do."

Returning back to England considerably sharper than when they had left, the band visited Keith Herd's Fairview Studio (located in his front room) to record *The Rise and Fall Of Bernie Gripplestone*, which, although it failed to gain commercial release at the time, saw the band wholeheartedly embracing the new psychedelic scene. A brief change of name to Treacle heralded more recordings at Fairview (but no releases), and once again

**Opposite page: Mick Ronson (photo by Barry Plummer)**

financial pressure forced Ronson to seek more gainful employment, this time as a gardener for the local council, restricting his guitar pyrotechnics to a couple of evenings a week.

Ronson's big break came when another inhabitant of Fairview, folk singer Michael Chapman, landed a recording deal with the Harvest label. Ronson was summoned down to London where he commenced to play blistering guitar on Chapman's *Fully Qualified Survivor* album.

Back home, The Rats finally decided to call it a day in January, 1970, after a storming gig at The Duke Of Cumberland in North Ferriby. Ronson briefly worked with a bunch of local lads under the name Ronno (they recorded one single in 1971, *4th Hour Of My Sleep* b/w *Powers Of Darkness* on Vertigo 6059029), but seemed resigned to a life with the local council. "There was something about it - cutting grass, pruning roses, I had sheep to look after too. I really enjoyed it. I thought maybe that's what I'd end up doing."

But once again fate was to play a hand. Former Rats' drummer John Cambridge was now working in London with a band called Juniors Eyes, who had landed a gig backing a promising singer cum songwriter called David Bowie. Bowie's one big hit from '69, *Space Oddity*, had been produced by Gus Dudgeon, who had also worked on the Chapman album. Dudgeon recommended the young guitarist to Bowie who, on discovering the connection with Cambridge, sent the drummer to Hull to bring Ronson back. Cambridge found Ronson marking out a rugby pitch and gave him the good news. Ronson, who had only recently paid off his debts from his days with The Rats, was initially sceptical, but then decided to give it a go. He debuted with Bowie on a *Top Gear* broadcast taped on the 5th of February, 1971, and the pair of them hit it off immediately. "I really liked David," he recalled some years later to Bowie biographers, Peter and Lenni Gillman. "It was real classy, it was different, I was in London, I was all set."

Over the next few years, Bowie, ably assisted by the Ronson led Spiders From Mars, proceeded to conquer the world (or at least the parts that mattered musically), with the guitarist playing on all of Bowie's waxings from '71's apocalyptic *The Man Who Sold The World* to '73's retro set, *Pin Ups*. After duetting *The Jean Genie* with Bowie on the latter's *Midnight Special* TV extravaganza, *The 1980 Floor Show* ("I turned up, put me make-up on, got me guitar out, played, put me guitar away, took me make-up off and went home"), Ronson was effectively out of the frame. Bowie opted to handle the guitar duties on his new album, *Diamond Dogs*, himself, as well as replacing the remaining Spiders with hired session men, leaving his trusty sideman effectively out on a limb.

Ronson's pedigree as an arranger and player was strictly first division (as well as the *Dudes* album, he had also worked on albums by Lou Reed and Dana Gillespie, plus Lulu's hit single, *The Man Who Sold The World*), and so it was no surprise to find his management considering the prospects of a solo career, particularly as Bowie had recently announced the first in what would become a long line of 'retirements'. It was duly announced, via a six storey billboard in New York's Times Square (costing $5,000 a week), that Ronson's debut album, *Slaughter On 10th Avenue*, would shortly be in the shops via the good people at RCA (even though it hadn't been recorded yet). "He was pushed into it by Tony and the MainMan machine," said his future wife Suzi Fussey, then employed as hairdresser to Mr. B. "It was a very hard thing to do after coming off something like David, and Mick wasn't ready."

Ronson himself was aware that he was being shanghaied, but gave in to the demands of his manager. "Tony de Fries had this idea that I was to become another David Cassidy or something like that. A total money making venture . . . "

The problem was that the venture failed to make any money at all. Both the album and its two singles, *Love Me Tender* b/w *Only After Dark* and *Slaughter On 10th Avenue* b/w *Leave My Heart Alone* failed to chart (despite *Circus* magazine, in a somewhat over the top feature, describing it as "an unexpectedly brilliant first LP"), and a U.K. tour was sparsely attended. Even so, RCA were talked into financing the recording of a second album, *Play, Don't Worry*, scheduled for release in February, '75.

**Opposite page: Mick Ronson (photo by Barry Plummer)**

In the meantime, smelling money, MainMan advised Ronson that it would be a smart move to take up Hunter's offer. It was agreed by both sets of managers that he could continue his solo career "whenever it didn't interfere with Mott's commitments", and, after a hurried rehearsal, he made his debut at the Olympen Theatre in Lund, Sweden, on the 10th of October, 1974. Hunter, at least, was overjoyed, saying at the time that "when Mick Ronson joined it was like a whole new band. I started writing again. Then we did this tour of Europe and the atmosphere got real strange, real hateful. Mick had all these ideas, and some of the other members of the band just looked at him with suspicion; 'Who's he?'"

One of Ronson's first ideas was a dramatic change of image for the band. Pictures taken at the time, show a marked reduction in hair length (including the already balding Fisher, who was now made to go without his, up to now, trademarked hat). Buffin for one was resentful about what he saw as an intrusion into individual choice. "Ronson courted Ian, rubbished Watts, Fisher and me - got Ian, Watts and Fisher to have their hair chopped and other things." The drummer later let rip by adding that "he treated us like nuisances, irritations. He was never friendly."

Tapes from the Lund gig show the band mellowing out a little with plenty of slow numbers (much to the disgust of the audience who keep on calling for *Marionette* throughout - "We ain't doing it", is Hunter's terse reply) and a couple of new tunes thrown in for good measure. Ronson's occasional strangled solos were, unlike Bender's, limited to the odd song and his playing is, as usual, concise and economical, dominant without - as Bender tended to do - resorting to flash. The set was as follows: Intro (*American Pie*), *The Golden Age Of Rock'n'Roll*, *Sucker*, *Roll Away The Stone / Sweet Jane*, *Rest In Peace*, *Born Late 58* (featuring a tortured axe wank from the new boy which totally ruins the song's ending), *One Of The Boys*, *All The Way From Memphis*, *Rose*, *Saturday Gigs* (at the time not released), *Angel #9* (Ronson had helped out The Pure Prairie League on some arrangements and had decided to record this song, written by the band's Craig Fuller, for his second album. Their *Leave My Heart Alone* was issued as a b-side. This portion of the show replaced Bender's solo spot, and the rest of the band back him admirably), *Drivin Sister*, *The Crash Street Kidds* (a wild rendition featuring some heavy duty solos and a manic synth-organ ending from Fisher and Weaver), followed by a three song encore comprising of *Violence*, *All The Young Dudes* and a new song from the pen of Hunter, *Lounge Lizard* (introduced by Hunter as "a dirty, greasy rock'n'roller"), which had at the time got no further than the demo stage. Considering the lack of rehearsals, Ronson handles himself well throughout (his backing vocals are especially strong), although it's fair to assume that he already knew his way around the *Dudes* material, which made up 25% of the set. Indeed, if there is one criticism to be levelled at the band, it was their over reliance, from the summer of '72 onwards, on the *Dudes* album as a source of live material, particularly in the light of some of the excellent songs they cut in the following two years. Great tunes like *Honaloochie Boogie*, *I Wish I Was Your Mother*, and *Alice* never received a live airing, while one of their most popular songs, *Marionette*, was dropped from the set after the U.S. tour.

The tour, supported by long forgotten would-be pseudo heavy rockers, Titanic, rolled on into Denmark, Switzerland, Holland, Belgium, Liechtenstein, Germany and France, before finally coming to rest back in the Netherlands on the 3rd of November for a gig at Amsterdam's Concertgebouw, by which time the band had both a new album and single in the shops. CBS eagerly awaited their return to Britain and the commencement of a sizeable 29 date tour which, in pre-MTV days, was still the most effective way of selling your product to the masses. The failure of *Foxy Foxy* was forgotten. It was time to get back on the bandwagon.

*"It seemed real good for about a week . . . it all seemed like everybody was enthusiastic but after a few days it was a drag really . . . they were together for a long time and then, when they got a little money, not a lot of money but a little bit, they didn't want to pour any of it back into the band . . . they didn't want to gamble. To them it was a steady job."*

*MICK RONSON.*

*"Ronson wouldn't BE one of the group. He wouldn't talk to us . . . we had a guitarist who wouldn't socialise or talk or eat with us. On the final Mott The Hoople tour, the hotels we stayed in were so expensive we couldn't afford to eat in them, usually necessary due to tight schedules. All of us, except Ian and Ronno, used to trudge off with the road crew in search of an affordable meal. We would have eaten with Ian and Mick if we'd had the money. They never joined us in the cheap cafes."*

*BUFFIN.*

## CHAPTER

# 21

The introduction of Ronson into the ranks, which initially looked like a blessing, turned out to be more of a curse. While the guitarist always maintained that he wanted to fit in with the band, it was obvious that this wasn't going to be a marriage made in heaven. Hunter was becoming bored with the album-tour grind and the pressures of coming up with a couple of hit singles every 12 months, and in Ronson he saw something of an ally, a guitar for hire, always willing to experiment, and not shackled to the Top 40 treadmill. It was inevitable that tensions would emerge and sides taken, a point noted only too well by Morgan Fisher. "Obviously, he had a great track record with Bowie and stuff, but somehow there were personality clashes. I sort of felt myself in the middle of it, between the Buffin / Overend axis and the Ian / Mick axis, which was more American orientated. I felt in the middle because I hadn't been there from the beginning anyway, but there was definitely a divided band there, and it didn't take long for it to fall apart."

It was clear that Ronson was of the opinion that the rhythm section were just along for the ride, always ready for the easy option and unwilling to take chances. Certainly, in terms of songwriting, their input was minimal, but both had recently begun to get interested in the production side of things, and their commitment to live work (we're talking here about a band who hardly ever took a holiday in their entire career) was above question. As musicians they were solid and reliable, particularly Watts, who as well as being a fine bass player, could handle the guitar with ease, and of who his partner in rhythm once said that "Watts has never been given his dues as a musical influence on or within Mott The Hoople."

It seemed that Ronson, used to working in the highly charged arena of the Bowie camp where he had a big say in what went down musically, was unable to tolerate the more laid back approach of messrs Watts and Griffin. His opinion of Fisher is unrecorded (the

95

**Above: Mott The Hoople (photo courtesy of CBS)**

pianist's later solo projects showed him to be the most radical of the bunch, an avant-gardist on par with Brian Eno) while it was plain as day that he was full of admiration for Hunter, who he saw as the creative genius behind the band. In an interview published in the American rock mag *Circus,* he laid it on the line regarding his time with the group, pulling the minimal amount of punches. "It was really a bad trip. They're not a band. Just people who play to satisfy their egocentrism . . . I needed a band, but I soon realised that things weren't good. We played together on stage, but offstage everyone was on his own. They just didn't speak to each other. The last tour they did was not for the pleasure of playing live, making the crowd happy . . . they played just to make money for Christmas. They simply needed money to buy Christmas presents. How could I play with people like that?"

These comments are obviously in direct contrast to Buffin's assertion that Ronson hung out with Hunter but wasn't interested in the rest of the band. Indeed, Hunter had contributed backing vocals to Ronson's forthcoming album, which had been put on hold while he toured with Mott, and their friendship, *Dudes* sessions aside, developed from there. Ronson expanded on his theories when he told *Melody Maker* that "I enjoyed the idea of joining Mott. I thought it was all going to happen. But I was surprised after being with Mott The Hoople for a month and in the end I was getting disgusted by the behaviour of the band. They wouldn't come to sessions - I couldn't stand it. I felt all this as soon as we did the first gig.  As soon as we started playing gigs I knew what was going on, and it was ridiculous."

As far back as '72, Verden Allen was griping about the fact that in the studio "Buff was always reading and Pete would be there and they'd say 'Have we got it together yet?'", which hints at a lack of creative input, while in his book, Hunter chastises Watts about the fact that "given a week's holiday he still gets to rehearsals two hours late, and we have them a quarter of a mile from his place in Hampstead" (he also reckoned that the bassist "can sleep 14 hours a day when he's not working"), which goes a long way to explaining the rift that appeared in the band.  Griffin and Watts had spent over ten years playing together, a fair chunk of them in the confines of the group, while Ronson had been used to working with a vast array of artists whose repertoires encompassed a wide and varied set of musical styles.  As for Hunter, it was obvious that he was becoming restless, and the arrival of Ronson only heightened his wanderlust.  The cracks were beginning to appear.

*"I was very wild on stage, and offstage too. I was always drinking too much. Those days of whisky, wine - too much drinking. But no drugs. I don't think Mott The Hoople ever did drugs."*

*MORGAN FISHER.*

*"We were pre-punk punks. In a way that was the problem with Mott. We were never really in tune with what was going on. I didn't know at the time how much influence we had on people. Mott The Hoople was a very intense, emotional band. Everything was a big deal. Everything mattered so much. That's just part of growing up and being British, I suppose."*

*MICK RALPHS.*

## CHAPTER 22

The *Live* album was released by CBS at the beginning of November, complete with blurb from Stateside Columbia about it representing "their finest hour" (plus a promise that the band would be touring in April, May and June, '75), although it was pretty obvious to all concerned that it failed to fully capture the excitement and emotion that the band generated on stage. The sound quality was poor, the mix was hit and miss (Bender's guitar is right up front, giving it the air of a heavy metal concert), there's too much between songs banter (particularly during *Angeline*, which featured the full nine yards of Hunter's sexist barroom bullshit), while the set list struggled to give the listener the full spectrum of Mott's recorded output, but in doing so forced a compromise with an extremely hurried medley. Side 1 was taken from the Broadway show and featured *All The Way From Memphis, Sucker, Rest In Peace, All The Young Dudes* and *Walking With A Mountain*, while side 2 comprised of songs from the December '73 Hammersmith gig, and featured *Angeline, Rose* and a medley of *Jerkin Crocus / One Of The Boys / Rock'n'Roll Queen / Get Back / Whole Lotta Shakin' Goin' On / Violence*.

Buffin, on whose shoulders the responsibility of producing the album had fallen, remembered that "CBS would not go for a double - or have a bonus 10" - so the choice of material was pruned to fit. German CBS wanted *Marionette* for instance. It would have been nice to start with the *American Pie / Golden Age* coupling . . . *Live* was still quite long, and an L.A. cutting lab boasted they'd 'make the hottest cut we ever heard'. Heller offered to fly me and my wife to L.A. for the cut . . . it was crap and was finally made in London by Ray Staff at Trident."

Bootleg tapes in circulation today show that there were far better performances floating around in the cassette racks of Mott fans. The venues may not have been as prestigious (Bristol, Santa Monica and The Tower Philly are a few that spring to mind), but at the end of the day the listener is interested in the performance and the sound quality, not where it came from. Many fans felt the band should have included live tapes from their entire career (à la Roxy Music on their excellent live album), and it would certainly have been interesting to hear the band represented over a five year period (the Fairfield Halls gig that spawned the live cut on *Wildlife* would have been a belter), spread over the wide canvas of a double album, which was a pretty standard format for rock bands in the early

Seventies. But as Buffin noted, record company and management bigwigs conspired against him, which, coupled with the apparent lack of interest from Hunter (who at the time was suffering from something of a creative drought) meant that the album turned out to be a major disappointment. (Note for trivia buffs: in 1988, the American radio show *The King Biscuit Hour* aired the Broadway show in full and, inevitably, bootlegs appeared, many far superior to the official product).

Buffin later recalled that "to the best of my recollection, the Uris show was only recorded once. I don't recall having a choice of tracks. Hammersmith had both shows (one day) recorded which allowed us the 15+ edits in a short section of the 'rock medley'. Also, the live Uris is edited out of real-time sequence for programming considerations. I think that CBS did a deal with KBFH to pay for the recording whilst CBS retained the rights to the master. You can see the stupid way our management and record company 'planned' things. Nobody records ONE night only of a seven day run. We did! And did they film / video the event - or even dress rehearsal? No, nothing."

Facing Ronson's on / off arrangement with the band, and Hunter's growing reluctance to pander to the Top 40 market, it had been decided by all to have one last crack at the singles market, mainly at the instigation of Buffin, who was unhappy with the session that had led to Bender's dismissal. "We were all frustrated with Bender's lack of input - none more so than Ian. I was unhappy to have *Foxy Foxy* as Mott's final single and tried to persuade Ian that we should put out a proper final single. He was unenthusiastic. I convinced CBS that I thought we had a great song - we had nothing. I plotted with Morgan and Overend to get the band into the studio to do a ghastly song that I had written called *Sunset Summer Nights*, as the final Mott single. We recorded the back-track; we even got Howie Casey to do the sax part and solo on it. All the while Ian looked more troubled as the rest of us enthused over this 'wonderful' song. Halfway through putting my guide vocal line on to the back-track, Ian said 'I've got an idea for a song', motioned us over to the piano and began to play the first draft of *Saturday Gigs*."

**Below: Ian Hunter (photo by Barry Plummer)**

Listening to the tapes of that first tentative run through today (with its lines about "69 was Safeways wine", "take the mick out of *Top Of The Pops* 'cos too much energy's a drag", plus the mix up about the year "we went to Croydon" . . . Hunter reckoned it was '73), it's clear that the shaded one had decided to call it day, what with his potted history of the band and 'goodbyes' sprinkled like confetti all over the fade.

The single had been issued just prior to the European dates and was included in the live set, along with another new Hunter tune, *Lounge Lizard*, both of which featured Mick Ronson. The 45 was issued by CBS throughout Europe, although, like its predecessor, not in the States, where, with the exception of the *Dudes* 45, the band were looked upon more as an FM radio act. But once again it failed to chart, heightening the feeling of despondency in the band and the pressure on Hunter, who was looking at a bridge too far in terms of commitment, with the inevitable results. The pressure, brought on by the shortfall of songs, hits, problems with Ronson, and general lack of assistance from his management, culminated in the inevitable crack-up and resulted in the singer being hospitalised. All future commitments were put on hold.

CBS quickly got wind of Hunter's discontent with the band and, viewing him as the most marketable commodity within the group, dangled the prospect of a solo deal. He accepted and the rest of the band were duly informed, much to their disbelief. Overend Watts remembered that "we did split up . . . and there was a tour coming up and we weren't able to fulfil it. We didn't know what to do as it was so sudden, it didn't happen over a period of time. So suddenly there was Buffin, Morgan, Blue and myself, and I started writing songs with Blue."

The relationship proved to be short-lived as Weaver received an offer of alternative employment. Watts recalls that "Blue came up to me one day and said he'd had an offer from the Bee Gees and didn't know what to do - it was £200 a week. With a wife and kids to support I told him that he had to do it."

Watts' advice proved to be spot on. Weaver, afforded songwriting credits by the brothers Gibb, enrolled just prior to the *Saturday Night Fever* album - a smart move by any standards.

Buffin remembered the harsh reality of the split. "When the call came from Ian that ended his association with the group, the pay stopped, and our bank balances were zero. Just like they had been in 1969. And there was no financial pay off, just mountains of debts."

The weekly wage was £75 per week, the debts immeasurable. Hunter burned his bridges, teamed up with Ronson (who was not affected as he was signed to MainMan), leaving the remainder of the band whistling in the wind. The rest, as they say, is history . . .

*"We never seemed to get it right somehow. We were always pissing somebody off. Now people realise that we were innovators."*

*IAN HUNTER.*

*"I'm afraid I never felt that Mott without Hunter had much chance."*

*MORGAN FISHER.*

**CHAPTER**

# 23

"After a while it was getting a bit too much in Mott. They all got a bit lazy and were relying on me too much. So I rang them up and I thought they'd know but they didn't. So that was a bit of a shock to them and me . . . and there I was, sitting on a bed talking to a doctor, as if he was the only friend I had in the world. Great bloke he was. They checked me over for physical stress, but couldn't find anything wrong . . . it was purely a mental condition, but it laid me out. There was a sold-out tour about to start, and I simply couldn't pull myself together to do it. This doctor said that if I didn't get away from it and re-think my life I'd be on my way to an early grave. I know that if I'd done that tour I'd have freaked uncontrollably."

So it was that with those words in November, 1974, Ian Hunter effectively killed off Mott The Hoople, opting instead for a solo career which invariably featured assistance from Mick Ronson until Mick's untimely death from cancer in 1993. Clutching a batch of songs written for what was to have been the next Mott studio album (which was tentatively titled *Weekend*), Hunter, with wife Trudi in tow, crossed the Atlantic to Weschester, NY, and the home of Blood Sweat & Tears sticksman, Bobby Colomby. There he was joined by Ronson, and Hunter worked up 11 songs (including *Lounge Lizard*, plus two other 'Hoople' non-starters, *One Fine Day* and *Coldwater High*), of which nine made it on to his debut album, released by CBS in March, 1975.

The rest of the band meanwhile opted to carry on, shortening their name to Mott and recruiting two new members - guitarist Ray Major and frontman Nigel Benjamin. Major was well known to Watts and Griffin as the guitarist with Hackensack, a minor league rock outfit signed to Island who had recorded a couple of albums (one of which featured *Movin On*, a Mick Ralphs' song rejected by Mott in '73 which also later appeared on the first Bad Company album) and of whom Overend Watts had nothing but praise, saying that, "He's a tasteful guitarist . . . he could be wild and looked good. He was a good bloke."

Watts also told the *NME* that "Buffin and me have been with Mott for six years or so, and we've got pride in what the band does. I mean, we could have reformed immediately after Ian left and done a tour of the States, just for the money. But it wouldn't have been any good and we'd have got labelled as Ian Hunter's old backing band, trying to make it without him."

The vocalist's shoes were filled by Nigel Benjamin, at the time gigging with Royce, who received a call out of the blue from an old friend. "She was in a call box and only had time to tell me to ring Stan Tippins before the pips went. Apparently she'd sent Mott some of my tapes without telling me, and they were very interested. I wasn't really thinking of joining another band at the time, I was quite happy with Royce, but I went down there all the same and after a couple of minutes I knew this was the band for me. We ended up recording three songs in about half an hour. It was really fantastic."

The band checked into Clearwell Castle in Gloucestershire and recorded their first album during May and June of '75. The record, *Drive On,* was released later that year to generally favourable reviews, particularly from *Record Mirror*, who wrote that "the excessive nostalgia of the old band's work has gone, and the result is an altogether fresher, brighter,

younger sound. Side 1 is brash, often jokey, and good. Side 2 is more serious, more confident and houses all of the albums best three tracks . . . all of which should be quite enough to persuade you to buy." Unfortunately, with the exception of die-hard fans of the band, very few neutrals were swayed, and the album stiffed in the shops.

The band, supported by the now long forgotten Upp, toured the U.K. in September, playing a series of well received (if not totally sold out) shows. The Hammersmith Odeon gig was a case in point, where the *NME* reviewer believed that "they've still got a way to go before they retain their old status, but everything's there waiting to be sifted through and worked upon. It's just a matter of time really."

Unfortunately time was the one thing that was in short supply. Still managed by Fred Heller in the States (he was also looking after Hunter), the band gigged heavily across the Atlantic both as a support and headline act and did well enough, but problems emerged when the band returned to the studio to attempt a follow up. "It was a difficult album to do", recalled Overend Watts. "Eddie Kramer (legendary engineer, famous for his work with Hendrix, Bowie and The Stones to name but a few) was supposed to produce it, but he came up and wasn't interested - and we really hadn't got the material together."

Released in June, '76, *Shouting And Pointing*, like its predecessor, failed to chart. Despite heavy gigging, supported by rockers Lone Star, plus a BBC *In Concert* radio broadcast aired on the 25th of October, the group failed to break through and, faced with the first wave of punk bands, struggled to find a market place for their hard driving (but somewhat pedestrian) songs. Inevitably, tensions within the band surfaced and towards the end of 1976 Benjamin (nicknamed 'The Dome' by the others behind his back) quit. Overend Watts later commented that "it was a pity when it came down to it that the musical ideas were different, he had the voice to do the sort of stuff we wanted to do - but in his own mind he wanted to be something more of a Peter Gabriel. Socially we got on well, he had a lovely sense of humour, but it was frustrating for him and he did actually leave the group of his own accord . . . "

The singer joined The English Assassins and later worked with The Little Roosters. In the mid-Eighties he relocated to L.A. in an attempt to forge a solo career, but was unsuccessful.

It was at this point that CBS decided to terminate the band's contract, leaving them without a label. Dissatisfied with the direction they were being led in, they split with manager Fred Heller, and signed to Colin Johnson of Quarry Productions, home of Status Quo. Johnson scored them a deal with Vertigo, Quo's label, and, now calling themselves The British Lions, they recorded a self-titled album, this time featuring the singing and writing talents of former Medicine Head singer-guitarist, John Fiddler. Watts remembered that "Morgan asked me one day why we hadn't asked John Fiddler to join us - after thinking about it, it occurred to me that he was a good writer and good singer as well - so we asked him. He was delighted when the subject was broached . . . "

The album disappeared without a trace in a British market now awash with angry young men talking 'bout their generation, and singing about violence and social unrest (just as Mott had done a couple of years earlier), but in the States, where it was released by RSO, it was given a big promotional push, shifting enough units to scrape into the lower end of the chart. Johnson was keen to capitalise on this success and promptly whisked the band across the Atlantic. Unfortunately, his knowledge of the U.S. concert scene was limited (Quo never managed to break through Stateside) and, as Watts recalls, the band ended up "playing all the wrong places and things got a bit grim. We were playing festivals in the middle of nowhere."

Despite this setback, the band returned to Britain and entered RAK Studios to record their second album, *Trouble With Women*, only to find that on completion Vertigo had decided against issuing it. With RSO following suit, the band had little option but to split, although the album did finally see the light of day in 1980 when it was issued posthumously in Britain by Cherry Red. Watts and Griffin drifted into production (as

Grimtone Productions), with the drummer later working as a house producer for Radio 1. John Fiddler joined Box Of Frogs for a couple of albums before embarking on a solo career, Major joined Partners In Crime and worked sessions, while Fisher embarked on a solo career which saw the release of a batch of weird and wonderful albums on Cherry Red (the most notable being *Sleeper Wakes*, *Hybrid Kids* and *Miniatures*), before forming Pipe Records as an outlet for his own, plus others, work. He kept his hand in playing sessions (for a while he was a member of John Otway's band, as well as working with ex-Bonzo Dog Neil Innes and playing keyboards for Queen on their 1982 European tour) and working as a producer, a role which eventually took him to Japan, where he carved out a successful career writing background music for films and TV as well as producing many of the Oriental bands that have sprung up over the last few years. Inbetween all this he still finds time to issue the odd solo album.

Over 20 years after splitting, the legacy of Mott The Hoople lives on. Numerous

**Above: Mott at Nigel Benjamin's 21st birthday party (photo by Barry Plummer)**

compilations plus cover versions of their songs have led people back to those early albums full of optimism, raw power and boundless energy, and to the conclusion that, yes, they really were a great band who never fully received the recognition they deserved. One can't help thinking that, afforded the promotional tools that today's rock bands receive (CDs, videos and MTV) Mott The Hoople, a band always strong on hooks and image, would have been massive. It's a thought that has crossed Ian Hunter's mind on more than one occasion, although the lure of the inevitable money spinning reformation has no appeal to him at all. "I don't know what it is we represent, but we most certainly do not want to cash in on our success . . . it would be the most ridiculous idea to reform Mott The Hoople. Well, actually we did it once. I can't remember where and when but it was a night full of bullshit. There was too much bitterness and disagreements."

Inevitable, I suppose, from a band who always truly BELIEVED in the power of rock'n'roll but in doing so always managed to keep their feet firmly on the ground. Also, as Dale Griffin honestly put it; "What's the point of 'All The OLD Dudes'?

INTEGRITY. That's the word.

# TOUR DATES

## 1969

6/8   BAT CAVERNA CLUB, Riccione, Italy (two week residency)
5/9   MARKET HALL, Romford
17/9  FILLMORE NORTH, Sunderland
7/10 SPEAKEASY, London
2/11 MAIDA VALE STUDIO, London (BBC session)
8/12 FRIARS, Aylesbury
14/12 GREYHOUND, Croydon
21/12 ROUNDHOUSE, London
31/12 NORTHCOTE ARMS, Southall

## 1970

1/1   FRIARS ADDISON CENTRE, Kempston, Beds
3/1   MOTHERS, Birmingham
4/1   CLOUD 9, Peterborough
8/1   WESTFIELDS COLLEGE, Hampstead
9/1   TEMPLE WARDOUR STREET, London
11/1 CHEESES, Stansted
12/1 WINTER GARDEN, Cleethorpes
15/1 PENTHOUSE, Scarborough
16/1 UNIVERSITY OF EAST ANGLIA, Norwich
17/1 UNIVERSITY OF SURREY, Guilford
18/1 GREYHOUND, Croydon
21/1 JOINTS, Wimbledon
23/1 DRIFTERS ESCAPE, Beaufort (S. Wales)
24/1 VICTORIA BALLROOM, Chesterfield
25/1 PIED BULL, Islington
26/1 LEYS YOUTH CLUB, Letchworth
29/1 OLD GRANARY, Bristol
31/1 LOUGHBOROUGH UNIVERSITY, Leicester
1/2   BLETCHLEY YOUTH CLUB, Bletchley
2/2   FRIARS, Aylesbury
3/2   MAIDA VALE STUDIO, London (BBC session)
4/2   TOP RANK, Leicester
5/2   STONEHENGE CLUB, Oxford
7/2   CHELSEA COLLEGE, London
12/2 EDEN PARK HOTEL, Beckenham
13/2 LEICESTER COLLEGE, Leicester
14/2 ALMA ROAD YOUTH CLUB, St. Albans
19/2 NEW PENNY CLUB, Watford
20/2 MAIDSTONE COLLEGE, Maidstone
21/2 UNIVERSITY OF NOTTINGHAM, Nottingham
25/2 BRISTOL UNIVERSITY, Bristol
27/2 WARWICK UNIVERSITY, Coventry
28/2 LONDON SCHOOL OF ECONOMICS, London
1/3   NORTHCOTE ARMS, Southall
2/3   KEELE UNIVERSITY, Stoke

3/3 NICKELODEON, Wood Green
4/3  NEW JOINTS, Wimbledon
6/3  FACTORY, Birmingham
7/3  IMPERIAL COLLEGE, London
8/3  MR. SMITHS, Manchester
10/3  BLIGH HOTEL, Sevenoaks
12/3  JIMMYS, Brighton
13/3  NEWCASTLE POLYTECHNIC, Newcastle
14/3  LEEDS UNIVERSITY, Leeds
15/3  ANGEL HOTEL, Godalming
17/3  DACORUM COLLEGE, Hemel Hempstead
19/3  BINGLEY COLLEGE, Bingley
20/3  GRAMMAR SCHOOL, Hartlepool
21/3  COUNTRY CLUB, Kirklevington
22/3  OSWALD HOTEL, Scunthorpe
24/3  BEAT CLUB, Bremen (TV show)
26/3  ELECTRIC CIRCUS, Lausanne, Switzerland (two nights)
1/4  VICTORIA HALL, Chelmsford
3/4  BLUESVILLE, High Wycombe
4/4  EEL PIE ISLAND, London
5/4  GEORGE HOTEL, Stoke
8/4  CASTLE, Tooting
9/4  LAFAYETTES, Wolverhampton
11/4  VAN DYKES, Plymouth
14/4  TOWN HALL, Watford
16/4  WINTER GARDENS, Weston-Super-Mare
18/4  BARN CLUB, Thaxted
19/4  NORTHCOTE ARMS, Southall
20/4  ROUNDHOUSE, London
22/4  TOWN HALL, Guilford
23/4  PARIS THEATRE, London (BBC session)
24/4  MEDICAL SCHOOL, Cleveland, Middlesex
25/4  NEWMANS TECH, Birmingham
26/4  GREYHOUND, Croydon
27/4  KINGSTON HOTEL, Kingston
28/4  CORN EXCHANGE, Cambridge
1/5  MARYLAND CLUB, Glasgow
2/5  C.F. MOTT TECHNICAL COLLEGE, Liverpool
4/5  FRIARS, Aylesbury
6/5  DULWICH HALL, London
8/5  COUNTRY CLUB, Hampstead
9/5  WATFORD TECH, Watford
11/5  COOKS FERRY INN, Edmonton
16/5  ROUNDHOUSE, Dagenham
29/5  EAST TOWN THEATRE, Detroit (two nights)
4/6  STATE UNIVERSITY, New York
5/6  ELECTRIC FACTORY, Philadelphia
10/6  FILLMORE EAST, New York (two nights / four shows)
13/6  CROSSLEY FIELDS, Cincinatti
15/6  Venue Unknown, Boston (three nights)
19/6  Venue Unknown, Porchester (two nights)
23/6  CONVENTION CENTRE, Fort Worth
24/6  HEMISPHERE ARENA, San Antonio
25/6  HOFHEINZ PAVILLION, Houston
26/6  ARACTON BALLROOM, Chicago (two nights)

1/7  HARVARD STADIUM, Cambridge, Mass
4/7  CONVENTION CENTRE, Asbury Park, NJ
5/7  ATLANTA POP FESTIVAL, Macon
6/7  WHISKY-A-GO GO, Los Angeles (two nights)
9/7  FILLMORE WEST, San Francisco (four nights)
16/7  SPECTRUM, Philadelphia
18/7  THE WAREHOUSE, New Orleans
19/7  Venue Unknown, Houston
21/8  MAYFAIR BALLROOM, Newcastle
22/8  BARN CLUB, Bishops Stortford
23/8  COATHAM ARMS JAZZ CLUB, Redcar
31/8  Venue Unknown, Canterbury
4/9  FLAMINGO BALLROOM, Hereford
5/9  ELM COURT YOUTH CENTRE, Potters Bar
11/9  PARADISIO CLUB, Amsterdam
13/9  FAIRFIELD HALL, Croydon
18/9  COUNTRY CLUB, Hampstead
19/9  LIVERPOOL STADIUM, Liverpool
21/9  COOKS FERRY INN, Edmonton
24/9  POLYTECHNIC, Manchester
25/9  POLYTECHNIC, Bristol
26/9  VAN DYKE CLUB, Plymouth

27/9 NORTHCOTE ARMS, Southall
29/9 TOWN HALL, High Wycombe
30/9 MARQUEE, London (also appeared on Disco 2)
1/10 McILROYS BALLROOM, Swindon
2/10 UNIVERSITY, Lancaster
5/10 CIVIC HALL, Dunstable
6/10 TOWN HALL, Birmingham
7/10 CASTLE, Tooting
9/10 BRUNEL UNIVERSITY, Uxbridge
10/10 COUNTRY CLUB, Kirklevington
11/10 WAKE ARMS, Epping
15/10 PENTHOUSE, Scarborough
16/10 EEL PIE ISLAND, London
17/10 ROUNDHOUSE, Dagenham
18/10 GREYHOUND, Croydon
19/10 OLD GRANARY, Bristol
20/10 RESURRECTION CLUB, Barnet
22/10 WINDRUSH CLUB, Reading
23/10 NORTHERN POLYTECHNIC, London
24/10 CREWE COLLEGE, Crewe
25/10 LYCEUM, London
6/11 SISTERS, London
8/11 LYCEUM, London
13/11 POPERAMA, Devizes
14/11 BROMLEY TECH, Bromley
15/11 PAVILLION, Bournemouth
21/11 READING UNIVERSITY, Reading
22/11 ROUNDHOUSE, London
25/11 TECH COLLEGE, Dartford
26/11 FRIARS ADDISON CENTRE, Kempston, Bedford
27/11 WESTFIELD COLLEGE, Hampstead
3/12 BLOW UP, Munich
4/12 ZOOM CLUB, Frankfurt
5/12 HIGH SCHOOL, Frankfurt
6/12 TV HALL, Stuttgart
9/12 YORK UNIVERSITY, York
10/12 PENTHOUSE, Scarborough
12/12 ELM COURT YOUTH CENTRE, Potters Bar
15/12 SOUTH PARADE PIER, Portsmouth
16/12 HERITAGE BALLROOM, Hitchin
18/12 COATHAM ARMS JAZZ CLUB, Redcar
19/12 LIVERPOOL STADIUM, Liverpool
21/12 TOWN HALL, Dudley
22/12 RESURRECTION CLUB, Barnet
26/12 TOWN HALL, Birmingham
27/12 GREYHOUND, Croydon

# 1971

8/1 KNUFFLESPLUNK CLUB, Welwyn Garden City
9/1 COUNTRY CLUB, Kirklevington
12/1 STARLIGHT, Crawley
15/1 EDINBURGH UNIVERSITY, Edinburgh
16/1 STRATHCLYDE UNIVERSITY, Glasgow
17/1 KINEMA BALLROOM, Dunfermline

19/1 MARQUEE, London
20/1 BIG BROTHER CLUB, Greenford (Australian TV)
21/1 VAN DYKE CLUB, Plymouth
22/1 EXETER UNIVERSITY, Exeter
25/1 TOP RANK, Swansea
27/1 ALBERT HALL, Nottingham
28/1 CITY HALL, Newcastle
29/1 CITY HALL, Sheffield
30/1 CITY HALL, Hull
31/1 ST. GEORGES HALL, Bradford
2/2 CIVIC HALL, Wolverhampton
4/2 TOWN HALL, High Wycombe
5/2 TOWN HALL, West Bromwich
6/2 MANCHESTER UNIVERSITY, Manchester
7/2 LYCEUM, London
12/2 TRENT POLYTECHNIC, Nottingham
16/2 KONSERTHUSET, Stockholm (Local radio broadcast)
17/2 STOCKHOLM UNIVERSITY, Stockholm
18/2 VAXJO UNIVERSITY, Vaxjo
19/2 Venue Unknown, Ljungskille
20/2 UPPSALA UNIVERSITY, Uppsala
21/2 CUE CLUB, Gothenburg
26/2 SISTERS, London
27/2 FARX CLUB, Potters Bar
2/3 CIVIC HALL, Tunbridge Wells
4/3 McILROYS BALLROOM, Swindon
6/3 SOUTH PARADE PIER, Portsmouth
7/3 TOWN HALL, Cheltenham
8/3 MAIDA VALE STUDIOS, London (BBC Radio 1 session)
12/3 SOUTHAMPTON UNIVERSITY, Southampton
13/3 IMPERIAL COLLEGE, London
14/3 BLACK PRINCE, Bexley
19/3 WINTER GARDENS, Blackpool
20/3 LEEDS UNIVERSITY, Leeds
21/3 COATHAM ARMS JAZZ CLUB, Redcar
25/3 LOCARNO, Sunderland
26/3 MAYFAIR, Newcastle
27/3 LANCHESTER COLLEGE, Coventry
28/3 FAIRFIELD HALLS, Croydon
3/4 LIVERPOOL STADIUM, Liverpool
4/4 PALACE THEATRE, Westcliff-on-Sea
9/4 MISTRALE CLUB, Beckenham
10/4 VILLAGE ROUNDHOUSE, Dagenham
11/4 DISCO 2 Recording
14/4 TOP RANK, Watford
15/4 GUILDHALL, Plymouth
17/4 WINTER GARDENS, Malvern
18/4 VICTORIA HALLS, Stoke
22/4 TOWN HALL, Birmingham
23/4 LOWESTOFT COLLEGE, Lowestoft
24/4 KINGSTON POLYTECHNIC, Kingston

The proposed U.S. tour with Free was cancelled at the last minute when the headline act disbanded, leaving the band with only a couple of dates on the board.
18/6 EASTOWN THEATRE, Detroit (two nights)

25/6  DURHAM UNIVERSITY, Durham
26/6  LEICESTER POLYTECHNIC, Leicester
1/7   TOP OF THE POPS (*Midnight Lady*)
3/7   PAVILLION, Felixstowe
8/7   ROYAL ALBERT HALL, London
9/7   KINETIC CIRCUS, Birmingham
10/7  SPA ROYAL HALL, Bridlington
11/7  FLORAL HALL, Southport
24/7  CITY HALL, Truro
25/7  GUILDHALL, Plymouth
30/7  TOWN HALL, Cheltenham
31/7  THE DOME, Brighton
7/8   TOWN HALL, Torquay
8/8   COMMON, Southsea
13/8  MAYFAIR, Newcastle
28/8  WEELEY FESTIVAL, Clacton
29/8  LYCEUM, London
30/8  HEREFORD TOWN FC, Hereford
4/9   TOWN HALL, Aylesbury
27/10 TOWN HALL, Oxford
30/10 ALBERT HALL, Nottingham
1/11  TOWN HALL, Birmingham
4/11  GREENS PLAYHOUSE, Glasgow
5/11  CITY HALL, Newcastle
6/11  CITY HALL, Hull
14/11 RAINBOW, London

# URIS THEATRE

RON DELSENER

*presents*

# MOTT THE HOOPLE

*with their very special guest*
# QUEEN

*Executive Producer:*
FRED HELLER

*Associate Producers:*
JONATHAN SCHARER                BOB HIRSCHMAN

21/11 CIVIC HALL, Guilford
22/11 COLSTON HALL, Bristol
25/11 GUILDHALL, Southampton
28/11 GUILDHALL, Plymouth
29/11 CIVIC HALL, Wolverhampton
9/12  DEUTSCHLAND HALLE, Berlin
20/12 CIVIC HALL, Wolverhampton
31/12 PARIS THEATRE, London (Radio 1 session)

# 1972

2/1   COATHAM ARMS JAZZ CLUB, Redcar
7/1   TOWN HALL, High Wycombe
8/1   WINTER GARDENS, Malvern
15/1  THE VILLAGE, Dagenham
20/1  WARWICK UNIVERSITY, Coventry
21/1  CHELSEA VILLAGE, Bournemouth
22/1  UNIVERSITY OF ESSEX, Colchester
29/1  WATFORD COLLEGE OF TECHNOLOGY, Watford
5/2   ROCK STREET CENTRE, Wellinborough
10/2  KELVIN HALL, Glasgow
11/2  BEACH BALLROOM, Aberdeen
12/2  EDINBURGH UNIVERSITY, Edinburgh
13/2  UP THE JUNCTION, Crewe
14/2  FREE TRADE HALL, Manchester
18/2  CITY HALL, Newcastle
19/2  LIVERPOOL STADIUM, Liverpool
20/2  FAIRFIELD HALLS, Croydon
25/2  LOCARNO, Sunderland
1/3   UNIVERSITY, Aberystwyth

26/3  Group travel across Europe to play in a converted gas holder on the outskirts of Zürich.  They split up but on return to U.K. find they are contracted to appear as part of the Rock'n'Roll Circus Tour.

5/4   GUILDHALL, Plymouth
6/4   CIVIC HALL, Wolverhampton
8/4   LIVERPOOL STADIUM, Liverpool
9/4   CIVIC HALL, Guilford
11/4  EMPIRE THEATRE, Edinburgh
12/4  GREENS PLAYHOUSE, Glasgow
13/4  CITY HALL, Newcastle
14/4  EMPRESS BALLROOM, Blackpool
15/4  MARKET HALL, Carlisle
16/4  VICTORIA HALL, Stoke
18/4  ST. GEORGE'S HALL, Bradford
19/4  LYCEUM, London
20/4  GUILDHALL, Portsmouth
21/4  COLLEGE OF EDUCATION, Luton
17/5  GRONA LUND, Stockholm
18/5  LISEBERG, Gothenburg
19/5  OLYMPEN, Lund
20/5  WAMOHALLEN, Karlskrona
21/5  W-DALA NATION, Uppsala
23/5  CULTURE HOUSE, Helsinki

24/5  CONCERT HALL, Abo
20/7  TOP RANK, Watford
21/7  TOP RANK, Doncaster
28/7  CITY HALL, Newcastle
1/8   COMMUNITY CENTRE, Slough
2/8   CIVIC HALL, Guilford
15/9  CIVIC HALL, Dunstable
16/9  FREE TRADE HALL, Manchester
17/9  VICTORIA HALL, Stoke
19/9  TOWN HALL, Middlesbrough
20/9  CITY HALL, Newcastle
21/9  TOP RANK, Sheffield
22/9  MAYFAIR CENTRE, Doncaster
23/9  LIVERPOOL STADIUM, Liverpool
24/9  MARKET HALL, Carlisle
25/9  CIVIC HALL, Wolverhampton
26/9  CITY HALL, Leeds
27/9  TOP RANK, Birmingham
28/9  LOCARNO, Coventry
29/9  TOP RANK, Bristol
30/9  WINTER GARDENS, Malvern
2/10  CENTRAL HALL, Chatham
4/10  TOP RANK, Brighton
6/10  DREAMLAND, Margate
7/10  SOUTHAMPTON UNIVERSITY, Southampton
14/10 RAINBOW, London (two nights)

A three week U.S. tour is cancelled due to visa problems.

27/10 COLLEGE OF PRINTING, London
18/11 TOWN HALL, Northampton
24/11 PALLADIUM, Hollywood
24/11 COLLISEUM, Hollywood
29/11 TOWER THEATRE, Philadelphia (Broadcast on local radio)
2/12  PALACE, Porchester NY
3/12  MUSIC FAIR, Valley Forge
6/12  CONVENTION HALL, St. Louis
11/12 EMBASSY, Fort Wayne
13/12 METROPOLITAN, Detroit
16/12 AUDITORIUM, Chicago
17/12 Venue unknown, Cleveland
20/12 Venue unknown, Scranton NJ
22/12 ELLIS AUDITORIUM, Memphis

# 1973

10/2  FRIARS, Aylesbury
17/2  BRADFORD UNIVERSITY, Bradford
19/2  TOWN HALL, Birmingham
22/2  GREENS PLAYHOUSE, Glasgow
24/2  EMPIRE, Edinburgh
25/2  CITY HALL, Newcastle
27/6  Venue unknown, Chicago
28/7  CLOVERLAND STADIUM, Cleveland
29/7  Venue unknown, Detroit

1/8   Venue unknown, Virginia Beach
3/8   FELT FORUM, New York
4/8   Venue unknown, Boston
7/8   Venue unknown, Pittsburgh
8/8   SPECTRUM, Philadelphia
10/8  Venue unknown, Portland
11/8  Venue unknown, Providence RI
12/8  ASBURY PARK, New Jersey
14/8  Venue unknown, Milwaukee
17/8  ELLIS AUDITORIUM, Memphis
18/8  Venue unknown, Fayetteville
19/8  Venue unknown, Washington DC
3/9   TOP OF THE POPS (*All The Way From Memphis*)
11/9  AQUARIUS THEATRE, Los Angeles (two nights of rehearsals)
13/9  NBC TV (Midnight Special)
14/9  PALLADIUM, Hollywood
15/9  CELEBRITY THEATRE, Phoenix
16/9  Venue unknown, San Diego
20/9  COMMANDOR BALLROOM, Vancouver
22/9  PARAMOUNT, Portland
23/9  PARAMOUNT, Seattle
25/9  Venue unknown, Denver
28/9  WINTERLAND, San Francisco (two nights)
3/10  MUNICIPAL AUDITORIUM, Chattanooga
4/10  MUNICIPAL AUDITORIUM, Atlanta
5/10  WPB AUDITORIUM, West Palm Beach
6/10  COLISEUM, Jacksonville
10/10 MUSIC HALL, Cincinnati
11/10 AUDITORIUM, Chicago
12/10 MASONIC TEMPLE, Detroit
13/10 JOHN CARROLL UNIVERSITY, Cleveland
14/10 MASSEY HALL, Toronto
16/10 AUDITORIUM, Rochester
17/10 KLEINMANS MUSIC HALL, Buffalo
18/10 SYRIA MOSQUE, Pittsburgh
19/10 OHIO STATE UNIVERSITY, Columbus
20/10 SHUBERT THEATRE, Philadelphia
21/10 SEATON HALL, South Orange
24/10 PALACE THEATRE, Providence RI
26/10 RADIO CITY MUSIC HALL, New York
27/10 ORPHEUM THEATRE, Boston
28/10 Venue unknown, Hartford
29/10 Venue unknown, Bethlehem
31/10 INDIANAPOLIS THEATRE, Indianapolis
1/11  CIVIC CENTRE, St. Paul
2/11  CIVIC CENTRE, Kansas City
3/11  CONVENTION HALL, St. Louis
4/11  MASSEY HALL, Toronto
12/11 TOWN HALL, Leeds
13/11 ST. GEORGE'S HALL, Blackburn
15/11 GAUMONT, Worcester
16/11 LANCASTER UNIVERSITY, Lancaster
17/11 LIVERPOOL STADIUM, Liverpool
18/11 VICTORIA HALL, Stoke
19/11 CIVIC HALL, Wolverhampton

20/11 NEW THEATRE, Oxford
21/11 GUILDHALL, Preston
22/11 CITY HALL, Newcastle
23/11 APOLLO, Glasgow
25/11 CALEY CINEMA, Edinburgh
26/11 OPERA HOUSE, Manchester
27/11 TOWN HALL, Birmingham
28/11 BRANGLYN HALL, Swansea
29/11 COLSTON HALL, Bristol
30/11 WINTER GARDENS, Bournemouth
1/12  KURSAAL HALL, Southend
2/12  CENTRAL HALL, Chatham
14/12 HAMMERSMITH ODEON, London (two shows)

# 1974

20/3  TOP OF THE POPS (*Roll Away The Stone*)
21/3  ST. GEORGE'S HALL, Bradford
22/3  DE MONTFORT HALL, Leicester
24/3  COLSTON HALL, Bristol
25/3  CITY HALL, Sheffield
26/3  FESTIVAL HALL, Paignton
27/3  WINTER GARDENS, Bournemouth
11/4  CELEBRITY THEATRE, Los Angeles
12/4  CIVIC AUDITORIUM, Santa Monica (two nights, four shows, broadcast by local radio)
14/4  WARNER THEATRE, Frensco
16/4  REGIS COLLEGE, Denver
17/4  MEMORIAL HALL, Kansas City
18/4  KEIL AUDITORIUM, St. Louis
19/4  FAIRGROUND APPLIANCE BUILDING, Oklahoma City
21/4  ST. BERNARD CIVIC, New Orleans
25/4  R.P.I., Troy NY
26/4  ORPHEUM THEATRE, Boston (two nights)
28/4  EXPOSITION HALL, Portland
1/5   HARRISBURG FARM, Harrisburg
2/5   AGRICULTURAL HALL, Allentown
3/5   KINGS COLLEGE, Wilkes Barre
4/5   PALACE THEATRE, Waterbury
5/5   CAPITOL THEATRE, New York (two days rehearsals)
7/5   URIS THEATRE, New York (six nights, two shows performed on 10/5 and 11/5.  8/5
show broadcast on radio)
14/5  Venue unknown, Boston
15/5  CONSTITUTION HALL, Washington DC
16/5  MUNICIPAL HALL, Charleston
17/5  FOX THEATRE, Atlanta
18/5  KNOXSVILLE COLISEUM, Knoxville
20/5  MASONIC TEMPLE, Detroit
21/5  AUDITORIUM THEATRE, Chicago
22/5  MILWAUKEE AUDITORIUM, Milwaukee
23/5  MORRIS CIVIC CENTRE, South Bend
24/5  SPORTS ARENA, Toledo
25/5  ALLAN THEATRE, Cleveland
26/5  MERSHON AUDITORIUM, Columbus
27/5  MASSEY HALL, Toronto
28/5  LONDON ARENA, London, Ontario

29/5  Venue unknown, Pittsburgh

30/5  SCHUBERT THEATRE, Philadelphia (two nights, two shows on 31/5)

2/4  CIVIC HALL, Richmond

19/6  TOP OF THE POPS (*Golden Age Of Rock'n'Roll*)

21/6  SEEHEIM TV STUDIOS (two days filming *Hits A Go-Go* for German TV show)

3/7  TOP OF THE POPS (*Foxy Foxy*)

5/7  BUXTON FESTIVAL, Buxton

6/7  PALACE LIDO, Douglas, Isle Of Man

10/10 OLYMPEN, Lund

11/10 SCANDINAVIUM, Gothenburg

12/10 KONSERTHUSET, Stockholm

14/10 FALKON, Copenhagen

16/10 ATSV-HALLE, Saarbrucken

17/10 AUSTELLUNGSHALLE, Stuttgart

18/10 VOLKHAUS, Zürich
19/10 VADUZERSAAL, Vaduz
20/10 CONGRESS HOUSE, Bern
21/10 BRIENNER THEATRE, Munich
23/10 ROMA, Antwerp
24/10 FOREST NATIONAL, Brussels
25/10 OFFENBACH STADTHALLE, Frankfurt
26/10 STADTHALLE, Heidelburg
28/10 NIEDERSACHSENHALLE, Hanover
29/10 NORDMARKHALLE, Rendsburg
30/10 MUSIKHALLE, Hamburg
2/11  OLYMPIA, Paris
3/11  CONCERTGEBOUW, Amsterdam

The band had been booked on an extensive U.K. tour with Sailor, but Hunter's hospitalisation meant that the dates were cancelled.  The gigs were as follows:
10/11 APOLLO, Glasgow
11/11 LEITH HALL, Edinburgh
12/11 CAIRD HALL, Dundee
13/11 MUSIC HALL, Aberdeen
15/11 TOWN HALL, Leeds
16/11 EMPIRE, Liverpool
17/11 PALACE THEATRE, Manchester
18/11 GUILDHALL, Portsmouth
19/11 WINTER GARDENS, Malvern
21/11 BRANGWYN HALL, Swansea
22/11 CAPITOL, Cardiff
23/11 ODEON, Taunton
24/11 WINTER GARDENS, Bournemouth
26/11 TOWN HALL, Birmingham
27/11 GUILDHALL, Preston
28/11 GLOBE THEATRE, Stockton
30/11 LANCASTER UNIVERSITY, Lancaster
1/12  HIPPODROME, Bristol
4/12  GAUMONT, Ipswich
6/12  HAMMERSMITH ODEON, London (two nights)
8/12  CITY HALL, Newcastle
10/12 GAUMONT, Southampton
11/12 NEW THEATRE, Oxford
12/12 CIVIC HALL, Wolverhampton

Initially, when Hunter fell ill, it was thought that most of the tour could be salvaged, as at the time the band's management were unaware that he was on the verge of quitting.  The Scottish dates were therefore re-scheduled.

16/12 LEITH HALL, Edinburgh
17/12 CAIRD HALL, Dundee
19/12 MUSIC HALL, Aberdeen
20/12 APOLLO, Glasgow

# RECORDED OUTPUT

The bands early recorded output was subject to sporadic releases outside the major markets (U.K. & U.S.), and it wasn't until they signed to CBS that their work became more widely available throughout Europe and the Far East. What follows is a discography of U.K. releases only.

## SINGLES

Rock'n'Roll Queen / Road To Birmingham (Island WIP6072) 1969
Midnight Lady / The Debt (Island WIP6105) 1971
Downtown / Home Is Where I Want To Be (Island WIP6112) 1971
All The Young Dudes / One Of The Boys (CBS S8271) 1972
Honaloochie Boogie / Rose (CBS 1530) 1973
All The Way From Memphis / Ballad Of Mott (CBS 1764) 1973
Roll Away The Stone / Where Do You All Come From? (CBS 1895) 1973
Golden Age Of Rock'n'Roll / Rest In Peace (CBS 2177) 1974
Foxy Foxy / Trudi's Song (CBS 2439) 1974
Saturday Gigs / Live Medley (CBS 2754) 1974

## ALBUMS

Mott The Hoople (Island ILPS 9108) 1969
Mad Shadows (Island ILPS 9119) 1970
Wildlife (Island ILPS 9144) 1971
Brain Capers (Island ILPS 9174) 1971
All The Young Dudes (CBS 65184) 1972
Rock'n'Roll Queen (Island ILPS 9215) 1972
Mott (CBS 69038) 1973
The Hoople (CBS 69062) 1974
Live (CBS 69093) 1974

After the group officially split there have been various compilations issued. Again, U.K. releases only are listed.

Shades Of Ian Hunter & Mott The Hoople (CBS 88476) 1980
Two Miles From Heaven (Island IRSP 8) 1980
All The Way From Memphis (Pickwick SHM 3055) 1982
The Collection (Castle CCSLP 174)
1988 Walking With A Mountain (Island IMCD 87)
1990 Retrospective (Columbia Legacy C2K 46973) 1993
Mott The Hoople & Steve Hyams (See For Miles SEACD7) 1993
Backsliding Fearlessly (Rhino R2 71639) 1994
Original Mixed Up Kids: The BBC Recordings (Windsong WINCD 084) 1996

**Mott The Hoople**

**Mad Shadows**

**Wildlife**

**Brain Capers**

**All The Young Dudes**

**Rock'n'Roll Queen**

**Mott**

**The Hoople**

**Live**

# BOOKS

Diary Of A Rock'N'Roll Star - Ian Hunter (Panther)

After being out of print for a criminally long period, the above book is now available again courtesy of Independent Music Press (ISBN 1 897783 09 4).  It can be ordered from any good bookshop, price £7.95.  In case of difficulty please write to Independent Music Press, P.O. Box 3616, London. E2 9LN. England.

# Thank You

S.T. Publishing began life in 1991 and remains the only publisher dedicated to street culture and street music. Many thanks for reading *All The Way To Memphis - The Story Of Mott The Hoople* and we hope you enjoyed it. As always, we welcome and appreciate your views and thoughts on our books. Our address is at the bottom of this page.

We are always pleased to hear from authors who would like to see their labours of love appear under the STP flag. Drop us a line if that's you.

If you would like a copy of our current catalogue please write in. All of our books are available from selected outlets and all good bookshops (and even some of the bad ones), and we also offer a bloody good worldwide mail order service. Two books that just might tickle your fancy are . . .

## *Crash Course For The Ravers - A Glam Odyssey*
by Philip Cato (ISBN 1 898927 65 0)
An essential guide to growing up to the sounds of Bowie, Roxy Music, Bolan and, er, The Bay City Rollers.

## *The Complete Richard Allen Volume Six - Demo, Glam, Teeny Bopper Idol*
(ISBN 1 898927 35 9)
The sixth and final volume in the Richard Allen which includes three more cult novels from the Seventies.

## S.T. PUBLISHING
The home of street publishing
P.O. Box 12, Lockerbie, Dumfriesshire. DG11 3BW. Scotland.